The **GUINNESS** Book of
Sea and Shore Birds

Britain's Natural Heritage

The GUINNESS Book of

SEA AND SHORE BIRDS

Linda Bennett and Michael Everett

Line drawings by Pamela Dowson

GUINNESS SUPERLATIVES LIMITED
2 CECIL COURT, LONDON ROAD, ENFIELD, MIDDLESEX

©Guideway Publishing Ltd 1982

Designed and produced by Guideway Publishing Ltd,
Willow House, 27-49 Willow Way, London SE26

Published in 1982 by Guinness Superlatives Ltd,
2 Cecil Court, London Road, Enfield, Middlesex EN2 6DJ

Guinness is a registered trademark of
Guinness Superlatives Ltd

Bennett, Linda
Sea and Shore Birds.
1. Shore Birds - Great Britain - Identification
I. Title II. Everett, Michael
598'.2941   QL690.G7

ISBN 0-85112-307-4

Printed and bound in Spain by Mateu Cromo Artes Gráficas, S.A. Pinto (Madrid)

Maps and illustrations on pp. 13, 16, 17, 18, 19: David Perrott

Topography of a bird (p. 39): Rob Hume

The publishers wish to thank the following for their permission to
reproduce the photographs: *Aquila Photographics:* 53, 65 (Horace Kinloch);
67 (S. C. Brown); 71, 127 (Eric Soothill); 77, 83 (J. B. Blossom); 91
(A. W. Cundall); 101 (Guy Huntington); 115, 131 (Dennis Green); 119 (H. A.
Hems). *Ardea London Ltd:* 55 (B. Sage); 61 (S. Roberts); 75 (John Gooders);
81, 97 (John Wightman); 89, 139 (Jack A. Bailey); 93 (Kenneth W. Finx);
105, 133 (André Fatras); 107 (G. K. Brown); 111, 129 (Richard Vaughan);
117 (David & Katie Urry); 121 (C. R. Knights); 137 (Leslie Brown); 145
(Peter Lamb). *Bruce Coleman Ltd:* 51 (Jan & Des Bartlett); 57 (Adrian Davies);
95 (Pekka Helo); 99 (Richard T. Mills); 109 (Dennis Green); 113 (Cyril
Laubacher); 125 (Jane Burton); 135 (Wayne Lankinen); 143 (Robert Gillmor);
149 (Bruce Coleman). *Roy Dennis:* 87. *Dennis Green:* jacket cover and 63, 69, 73,
79, 85, 123, 141, 147. *Nature Photographers Ltd:* 59 (Don Smith); 103 (Michael
Gore).

Front Cover: Gannets

Contents

Introduction

During the last ten to fifteen years, the sum of our knowledge of seabirds and shorebirds has increased enormously and, even as we write, we are aware of a great deal of research which is either in progress or is about to be carried out. It is probably true to say that our understanding of these birds has improved fourfold since the 1960s—and that seabirds in particular now have a following among professional and amateur ornithologists greater than that of any other group of birds, including birds of prey.

So writing this relatively short book on the birds of our coastal and marine habitats has not been an easy task. We have sought to produce an introduction to these birds and their way of life, setting them in the context of their habitats and also giving some thought to their conservation problems. Because this is essentially a book for beginners, it also includes a fairly lengthy section on birdwatching in general and coastal birdwatching in particular.

We have not aimed to produce either a comprehensive work on the coast or on coastal birds or, for that matter, a complete identification guide: our intention is to introduce our subject in summary form and point the reader in the direction of other more detailed works on various topics. We have listed these in the birdwatching section—many of them have provided the background information we have used here.

Co-authors work together in many different ways. In our case, we divided the book almost in half. Linda Bennett wrote the 'Selection of Species' section, including doing all the research for the maps here and elsewhere in the book, and compiled the section on ornithological and conservation societies. Michael Everett wrote the rest of the introductory text and the glossary.

The Origins of Our Coast

In geological terms, the coasts of Britain and Ireland are relatively young: their present, comparatively stable state has existed for not much more than 5000 years. The character of our seaboard is the direct result of the four great Ice Ages of the Pleistocene era, which began about one million years ago, with the last great glaciation occurring about 20 000 years ago. As the ice came south from the northern polar regions, it froze the seas to an extent which boggles the imagination. Sea levels dropped by as much as 150 feet (45 m) below those we know today, eventually to rise again when the ice retreated. It is predicted that there will be another Ice Age in due course, and thus we are currently in what is called an 'interglacial' period. Our coasts are still feeling the effects of the last Ice Age and, despite the relative stability of the last 5000 years, some long-term changes are still taking place. This includes movements of the land itself, perceptible enough for us to be able to calculate that the northernmost parts of our islands are rising and the southernmost parts sinking at a rate of about $\frac{3}{4}$ in (20 mm) every decade.

The depth of the sea and its salinity are results of the changes brought about by glaciation. Similarly, the movement of those vast, thick sheets of ice shaped the land—and formed the coasts. Where the advancing and, ultimately, retreating ice formed steep-sided valleys through hard rock, great sea lochs (and, in the extreme, deep fjords) were formed—so typical of the northern part of Britain. Similarly, the removal of softer rock by the ice created great cliffs and rocky headlands, rocky and sometimes precipitous islands of all shapes and sizes, and a remarkable variety of rocky islets and sea stacks, all of which have, in turn, been sculpted over the centuries by the action of the sea itself. In the shorter term, the action of the water is breaking down this rock into boulders and stones, eventually resulting in sand and mud which, finally, may become involved in the formation of estuaries.

Basically, major estuaries were formed when the ice scraped across huge areas that had become exposed as the sea fell away—areas which were flooded again when the ice retreated and the sea came back. Estuaries are affected by two tides a day, and the constant movement of the water over the intertidal zones (the areas between the

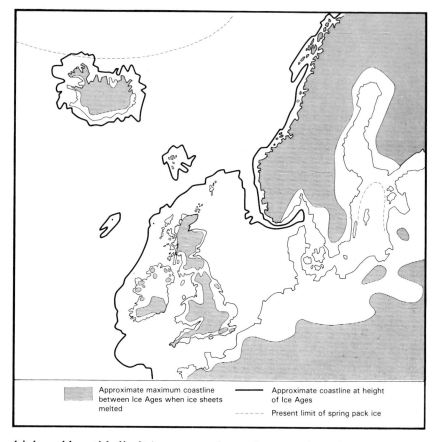

Approximate maximum coastline between Ice Ages when ice sheets melted

Approximate coastline at height of Ice Ages

Present limit of spring pack ice

high and low tide limits) creates a dynamic, ever-changing situation in which the erosion and deposition of material is a continuous process. Estuaries, therefore, are unstable and constantly—if, at times, imperceptibly—altering their shapes. The interaction of water and stones, sand and silt (which produces mud) results in a range of habitat types and, in the intertidal mudflat zone especially, exceptionally rich conditions in which salt-tolerant organisms can flourish—providing very good feeding for multitudes of birds.

There is often a very obvious natural succession of habitats—from the permanent water of an estuary to dry land. A sand or shingle spit is formed by deposition, with tidal mud on its landward side; plants colonise this mud and eventually form saltmarsh which, as it accretes (builds up and becomes higher), develops into meadowland. Man can alter the system still further by reclamation for towns, industry and agriculture, as well as by producing various kinds of effluents from his activities—all points we shall come back to later in this book.

The other major influence in an estuary is, of course, the freshwater input from its main river system, and the formation of strong, mixing currents produced when freshwater and saltwater meet. The flora and fauna of an estuary are determined by the combination of these effects—their presence, abundance and diversity differing in relation to wave action, currents, salinity levels and the supply of oxygen and nutrients. Interestingly, while some European rivers dominate the situation by carrying silt and other deposits down to the sea (and sometimes forming deltas as a result), in most of northern Europe, deposition is primarily from the sea.

So far, we can see that many factors have combined to produce the very varied conditions around our coasts which, as will be shown later, have given rise to superb opportunities for birds to feed and breed. Two more important factors must be taken into account when considering why it is that the coasts of Britain and Ireland are so exceptionally rich in birds. The first is our relatively mild winter climate which attracts vast numbers of wintering wildfowl and wading birds to our low-lying and food-rich estuaries, travelling from their breeding grounds which are as far away to the north as Greenland, Iceland, northern Scandinavia, Arctic Russia and Siberia. Secondly,

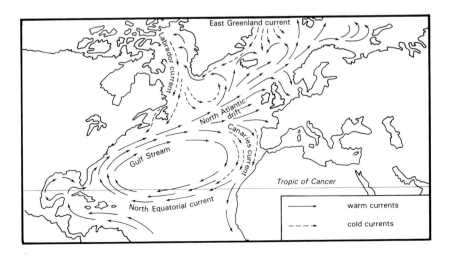

The currents of the North Atlantic.

our position on the north-western edge of continental Europe means that these islands are touched in parts of the north and west by the warm waters of the Gulf Stream, and they also lie within the ambit of that part of the North Atlantic where the warm waters of the North Atlantic Drift meet the cold currents coming down from the Arctic regions. It is the great turbulences and upswellings at the junction of these major currents which bring so many nutrients up from the deep, creating rich conditions in the sea in which marine organisms—plankton and krill—flourish, producing a rich harvest reaped by fish, birds, seals, whales and, ultimately, man himself.

Habitats

After our brief look at how our coasts have evolved, we must now examine the basic characteristics of the main habitat types and how these affect the birds which use them. All are affected to a greater or lesser extent by the sea itself, so it is logical to begin with this.

The Open Sea

As we have already indicated, the seas around our islands are particularly rich, due to the presence and junctures of ocean currents. The fact that most of the seas around the British Isles lie over a wide continental shelf, and are therefore shallow, enhances their productivity. There is a definite seasonal peak in this productivity—that is, in summer—and the 'true' seabirds, breeding in their huge colonies on cliffs and islands, time their breeding seasons accordingly and, depending on the species, either forage in inshore waters or feed far out to sea. In addition, these rich sources of food are partly exploited by visiting birds such as the great and sooty shearwaters which visit North Atlantic waters outside their own breeding seasons.

'True' seabirds are those which live at sea except for breeding.

In winter, food becomes far scarcer (although by no means non-existent) and seabirds scatter far and wide or move altogether to better feeding areas in other parts of the world's oceans. Some of these migrations are truly spectacular. Certainly the most famous is that of

14

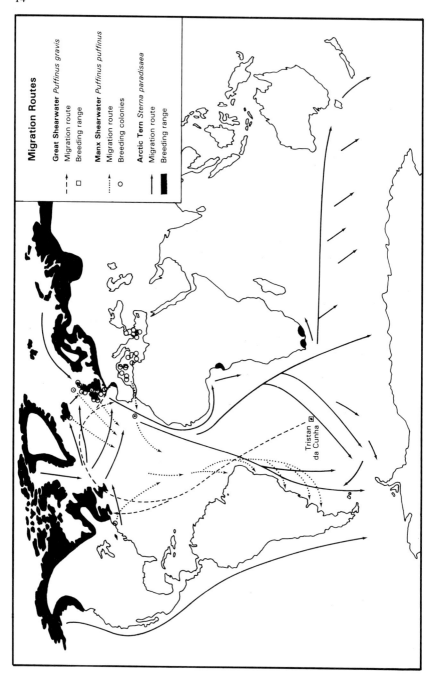

Migration Routes

Great Shearwater *Puffinus gravis*

- Migration route
- ☐ Breeding range

Manx Shearwater *Puffinus puffinus*

- Migration route
- ○ Breeding colonies

Arctic Tern *Sterna paradisaea*

- Migration route
- ■ Breeding range

Tristan
da Cunha

the Arctic tern, which journeys down to the Antarctic, but equally remarkable is that of the Manx shearwater, which circles the Atlantic as it flies down to its winter quarters in Brazil and then comes again to these shores.

Rocky Coasts, Islands and Stacks

Many truly seagoing species breed on the rocky coasts, islands and stacks which are predominantly in the north and west of our islands. A variety of species can utilise cliffs and stacks because, broadly speaking, they have subtly different nesting requirements and do not compete directly. The illustration on page 16 shows how a typical cliff might be apportioned, with gulls on the grassy tops—and shearwaters and petrels, too, coming ashore by night when predation risks are lowest—gannets on the tops and the upper slopes, guillemots on open ledges, kittiwakes on smaller outcrops and buttresses, fulmars mainly on vegetated ledges, razorbills in holes and crannies, and shags and black guillemots on the lowest, most broken sections. The sights and sounds (and smells) of a great seabird colony have to be experienced to be appreciated.

Cliffs and rocky shores support a very diverse fauna, varying according to exposure, wave action and climate, especially winter weather. These habitats are richest in south-west Britain and western Ireland where they are influenced by the Gulf Stream. Intertidal zones are relatively small, but little bays and beaches and complexes of pools and rocks exposed at low tide provide good foraging for many birds, especially waders such as oystercatchers and, mainly outside the breeding season, turnstones and purple sandpipers. Seagoing duck like eiders and red-breasted mergansers find good feeding just offshore.

Beaches, Spits and Shingle

A feature of some coasts are beaches, spits and shingle formed by deposition by the sea, their size and extent varying considerably according to wave action and, in some areas, the severity of winter storms. Some, like Orford Ness in Suffolk, are elongated spits which are growing continuously in length as more and more material is added; the great triangular shingle peninsula at Dungeness, Kent, is constantly being added to on one side, but eroded on the other. Stony beaches and spits and sandy beaches are all subject to a process known as 'longshore drift'. In nearly all coastal areas, waves strike the shoreline obliquely, rather than head on, but the water runs off more

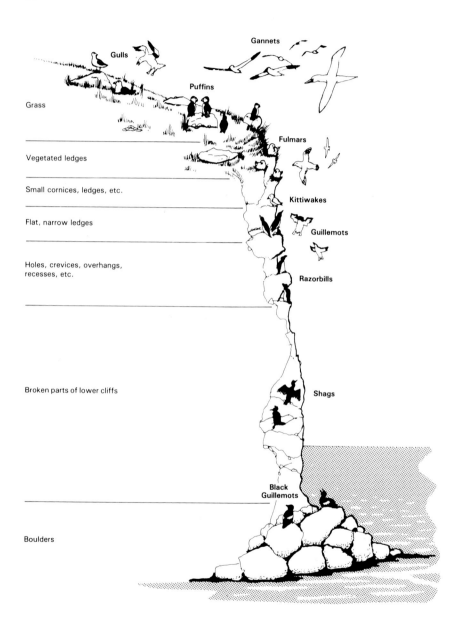

Gulls

Gannets

Puffins

Grass

Fulmars

Vegetated ledges

Small cornices, ledges, etc.

Kittiwakes

Flat, narrow ledges

Guillemots

Holes, crevices, overhangs,
recesses, etc.

Razorbills

Broken parts of lower cliffs

Shags

Black
Guillemots

Boulders

Seacliff nest-sites of different seabirds. This illustration shows the birds' typical
preferences, but usually there is also much overlapping between species.

or less at right angles to the beach; this results in the material deposited by the sea aggregating *along* the line of the beach, thus extending it laterally rather than towards the sea or inland. The higher and more stable parts of such beaches and spits soon become vegetated, and these often provide ideal nesting areas for colonies of gulls and terns and pairs of oystercatchers and ringed plovers. Sandy beaches shaped by longshore drift are frequently unstable in their natural state, depending on their steepness and exposure. However, man often stabilises them with moles, breakwaters, etc.

Intertidal areas of stony beaches and shingle, except where there are sheltered bays or extensive lee shores, are not particularly rich in food and generally only provide feeding for rather small numbers of birds. On the other hand, sandy beaches tend to provide somewhat better feeding conditions. This is particularly so where beaches are level and sheltered, and thus more stable, producing a good intertidal zone. Here, waders of many kinds find good pickings, in particular, species such as ringed plovers and sanderlings. Many waders also feed along the debris at the highest point of high tides, which characteristically form a marked ridge of plant litter and human rubbish along the upper beach. This narrow zone is often exploited most by small birds such as starlings, skylarks and pipits and, in winter, by flocks of finches and snow buntings. The upper reaches of sandy shores are seldom left alone by man for very long but, where there is less disturbance, ringed plovers breed and, importantly, colonies of little terns occur.

Sand blows off beaches and is deposited higher up in a pattern which bears a striking resemblance to that produced by waves on the shore. Where this occurs most markedly, sand dunes are formed by

The debris left by the tides at the highwater mark provides rich feeding for waders.

18

the wind, and like all the habitat types on low-lying coasts these are constantly changing and evolving, with erosion continually affecting the windward side and accretion compensating for this to leeward. Before long, the more sheltered parts are colonised by plants (especially marram) which, in time, serve to arrest and stabilise the dunes; man frequently makes use of planted marram to bind dunes and protect shorelines. Small, level valleys and slacks, often with shallow pools—and even small marshes in some areas—develop among the dunes. A few species breed in dune systems but these areas are generally rather poor for birds, although various passerines feed there, and when voles become numerous they may be hunted regularly by several species of birds of prey.

Machair

In a few areas, almost all in the Outer Hebrides and parts of western Ireland, shell-sand blown further inland has formed deposits over the existing rock to produce a grassy, flower-rich habitat known as *machair*. Because the calcium content of the shell-sand is so high, this is an exceptionally fertile habitat and has long been recognised as such by man; for example, it is no accident that, on the Outer Hebridean islands of North and South Uist, the fertile crofting land occurs down the western side of the islands, on the machair, and few people make their livelihoods on the acid, water-logged soils of the eastern side.

The fertile machair attracts many birds, particularly waders.

Machair is excellent for a variety of breeding birds, especially waders such as oystercatchers, ringed plovers and dunlin, and also contains superb shallow marshes abounding with waterfowl (even in winter) and waders, among which is the very scarce red-necked phalarope. Sadly, though, the effects of modern agricultural methods are slowly changing the face of the machair which must now be regarded as a threatened, if not vanishing, habitat in some places.

Estuaries

In the same way that Operation Seafarer (*see* page 49) provided invaluable data on breeding seabirds, the 'Birds of Estuaries Enquiry', carried out by the British Trust for Ornithology, the Royal Society for the Protection of Birds, the Wildfowl Trust and the Irish Wildbird Conservancy, has produced information on the numbers of waders and wildfowl using British and Irish estuaries. These data are not only fascinating in themselves but are of very considerable value to conservationists in assessing the importance of estuaries (which are threatened habitats) in national, European and international terms.

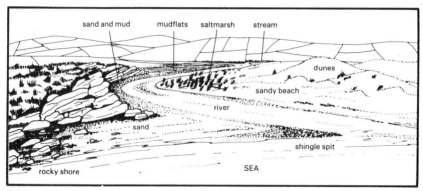

Profile of an estuary.

The map on page 22 shows those sites which regularly hold over 15 000 waders and/or 10 000 wildfowl; there are many more where numbers range from several hundred to several thousand. The two most important complexes are at Morecambe Bay, Lancashire, with a staggering average of close to *a quarter of a million* birds, and The Wash in eastern England with an average of 175 000.

Mudflats exist on all estuaries, varying considerably in their size and extent. Many estuaries have numerous, rather small areas of mudflats which are important in aggregate (the Firth of Clyde provides an excellent example of this), while others, such as the Thames estuary and Morecambe Bay, have vast, almost continuous areas of tidal mud. These differ not only in size but in the composition of the mud itself. Broadly speaking, the best mudflats are those made up of a mixture of sand and mud; these are the richest in oxygen and hold the greatest densities of invertebrates on which birds feed—a wide range of shellfish of varying sizes, worms, shrimps and so on, living on or just below the surface and exposed at low tide. This huge, varied food supply is exploited by many birds, including gulls and even crows, but principally by shelduck and wintering and migrant shorebirds.

Animal food is not the only kind exploited by birds; where the eelgrass *Zostera* is abundant, brent geese and, to a lesser extent, wigeon congregate in large numbers, feeding at low tide and even by moonlight. The 'Birds of Estuaries Enquiry' showed the importance of our estuaries for brents: more than a third of the world's dark-bellied brents wintering in Europe use the estuaries of the Essex coast, while over 25 per cent of the pale-bellied race winter on Strangford Lough in north-eastern Ireland.

Waders, often in vast scattered flocks, feed at low tide, and at high water form immense roosting flocks on nearby spits, beaches, saltmarshes and inland fields: few sights are as spectacular as a roost flock of several thousand oystercatchers, or a distant, midge-like cloud which contains 20 000 knot. It is, therefore, the state of the tide rather than the time of day which largely governs the movements of waders and other estuarine feeders. Waders are very variable in body size and structure, with differing leg lengths and bill lengths and sizes, so that, between them, the various species can exploit every source of food while minimising competition among themselves.

Plant colonisation primarily takes place above the intertidal zone, producing extensive saltmarshes as the main stage in the transition from the sea to dry land. Although they are above the reach of average tides, saltmarshes are frequently inundated by spring tides and lie on a substrate much influenced by saltwater, and therefore contain a range of salt-tolerant plants. Saltmarshes are characterised by systems of creeks and natural gutters which drain them, and very often by the presence of shallow pools. As a habitat for birds, salt-marshes provide good areas for breeding as well as for feeding and safe roosting at high tide. In winter, many passerine birds—especially finches—come from the land to feed on the abundant plant seeds, and these birds in turn often attract birds of prey such as hen harriers and merlins.

In some areas, large, uniform patches of the cord-grass *Spartina* are a dominant feature of saltmarshes; in its natural, original state this grass is actually rare, and the form we see today is the result of introduced species (by man for the purpose of stabilisation) producing a dominant, extremely hardy, hybrid form which is a rapid colonist, even of bare mud. However, it can cause problems, because it takes over more diverse and more desirable habitats.

Beyond the saltmarsh lies the grassier, much less salty, fresh-water-influenced grass marshland or 'grazing marsh', which provides important nesting areas for many wetland and coastal birds but which is a fast-dwindling wildlife resource as it is drained, further reclaimed and 'improved'; it is all too often the first area to be developed for building and industry.

Interestingly, the coastal habitats which are dominated by industry or urbanisation need not be poor for birds, even if they have taken the place of rather more interesting areas. Useful fragments of saltmarsh and a fringe of intertidal mud often remain and some birds, most notably gulls, are quick to exploit man's rubbish tips. Sewage outfalls often provide excellent feeding for birds, as at Edinburgh where, until fairly recently, over 30 000 scaup were sometimes present in winter—by far the greatest concentration around our coasts and up to one-third of the entire European winter population. Other seaduck, such as goldeneye, have benefited where grain from distilleries has been discharged into estuarine waters. Obviously, the presence of industry and large conurbations can also be harmful: quite apart from the destruction of natural habitats, there is all too often environmental pollution on a chronic scale.

Main Seabird Colonies and Estuaries for Waders and Wildfowl

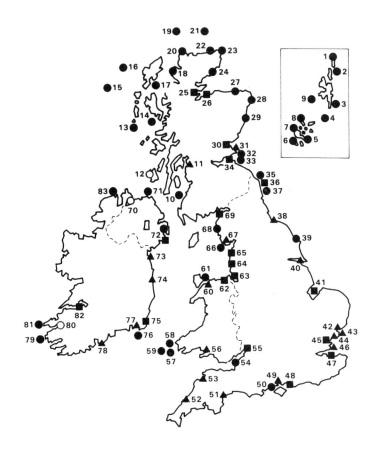

● Main seabird breeding areas
  (containing more than 10 000)

■ Main estuaries for waders
  (over 15 000) and wildfowl
  (over 10 000)

▲ Important estuaries for waders
  (over 15 000)

○ Important estuaries for wildfowl
  (over 10 000)

1	Hermaness	44	Hamford Water
2	Fetlar	45	Blackwater
3	Noss	46	Dengie Flats
4	Fair Isle	47	Thames (including Swale, Medway, North Kent Marshes, inner Thames and Foulness)
5	Copinsay		
6	Hoy		
7	Marwick Head		
8	Westray and Papa Westray	48	Chichester, Langstone and Portsmouth Harbours
9	Foula		
10	Ailsa Craig	49	Southampton Water
11	Inner Clyde	50	Needs Oar Point and coast westwards
12	Loch Indaal and Loch Gruinart, Islay		
		51	Exe
13	Berneray and Mingulay	52	Camel
14	Rum (Rhum)	53	Taw/Torridge
15	St Kilda	54	Flat Holm, Steep Holm and Stert Island
16	Flannan Islands		
17	Shiant Islands	55	Severn
18	Handa	56	Burry Inlet
19	Sula Sgeir and North Rona	57	Skokholm
20	Clo Mor	58	Skomer
21	Sule Skerry and Sule Stack	59	Grassholm
22	Dunnett Head	60	Conway Bay
23	Duncansby Head	61	Puffin Island
24	Berriedale and south towards Ord of Caithness	62	Dee
		63	Mersey
		64	Ribble
25	Cromarty Firth	65	Morecambe Bay
26	Moray Firth	66	Walney Island
27	Troup Head and Pennan Head	67	Duddon
		68	Ravenglass
28	Buchan Cliffs	69	Solway
29	Fowlsheugh	70	Lough Foyle
30	Firth of Tay	71	Rathlin Island
31	Eden	72	Strangford Lough
32	Isle of May	73	Dundalk Bay
33	Bass Rock	74	North Bull
34	Firth of Forth	75	Wexford Harbour and Slobs
35	St Abb's Head		
36	Lindisfarne	76	Saltee Islands
37	Farne Islands	77	Bannow Bay
38	Teesmouth	78	Ballymacoda Bay
39	Bempton Cliffs	79	Great and Little Skellig
40	Humber	80	Castlemaine Harbour
41	The Wash	81	Blasket Island
42	Stour	82	Shannon/Fergus
43	Colne	83	Horn Head

The Birds of Sea and Shore

In a later section of this book, we have selected a representative cross-section of 50 species from the many birds associated with the habitats we have described. Now we take a broader look at the main groups of birds involved, and consider the various ways in which they have adapted to life on, over or beside the sea.

Divers

Divers are long-bodied and long-necked, superb swimmers and strong fliers, but are almost helpless on land. As their name implies, they feed underwater, diving from the surface in search of fish. Our two breeding species, the red-throated diver and the black-throated diver, nest on inland waters but often feed on the sea, doing so almost entirely during the winter. The larger great northern diver is essentially a winter visitor from Iceland (some occasionally come in summer and there is one recent Scottish breeding record), while the white-billed diver is a very rare but regular wanderer from Arctic Russia.

Grebes are similar to these divers in many ways, but are smaller, with lobed rather than webbed feet. They likewise hunt underwater, but take a range of smaller prey. Three of our five species—Slavonian, great crested and red-necked—winter wholly or partly in inshore waters, although the red-necked, in fact, is relatively inland.

Two more birds which dive from the surface and feed on fish are the cormorant and the shag; both breed colonially on cliffs and sea islands. While the shag is a coastal species mainly of the north and west, the cormorant occurs more or less all around our shores and in some areas is not at all uncommon inland. Where they are present together, these two birds take different sizes of fish and thus do not compete directly for food.

'True' Seabirds

A whole group of 'true' seabirds ranges far out to sea in search of food and, indeed, they spend most of their lives well away from land, coming ashore only to breed. Fulmars are the nearest thing we have in the Northern Hemisphere to the much larger albatrosses of the southern oceans—superb seagoing gliders which feed on the surface and are

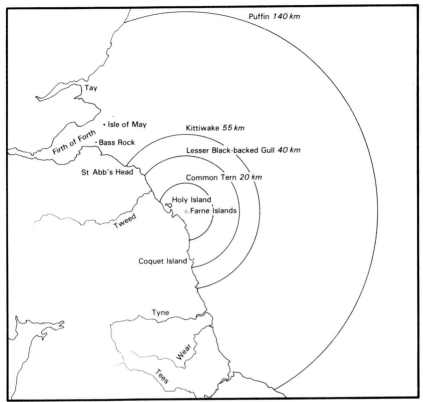

The feeding ranges of different seabirds. (Source: T.H. Pearson, 1968.)

also efficient marine scavengers. Shearwaters are similar in many ways, feeding mainly from the surface and travelling with a distinctive pattern of flapping and gliding as they use the wind and updraughts from the waves. Manx shearwaters breed here and winter out in the Atlantic, while three other species are regular visitors outside their own breeding seasons, appearing in British and Irish waters from late summer into autumn. Cory's shearwater is the scarcest and breeds in the Mediterranean and on the islands off north-west Africa; sooty shearwaters come from the Southern Hemisphere, as do great shearwaters which nest on islands in the South Atlantic and move in an immense clockwise loop around the Atlantic after the breeding season.

Petrels, like shearwaters, come ashore to their breeding areas at night when predation is less likely. Our two species are both small, deceptively frail-looking birds which are actually great seagoers, skimming and fluttering low over the waves and picking up small food items from the surface. Storm petrels not infrequently follow ships—like many seabirds, they profit from the disturbance caused by passing ships which brings a great deal of small prey up to the surface. Gannets are our largest seabirds, long-range fishermen with magnificent powers of flight. They breed on cliffs and sea stacks in huge colonies and many travel considerable distances in search of food, fishing by plunging headlong into the sea, sometimes from as high as 100 feet (30 m).

All seagoing birds are affected by the wind, and severe weather may cause them problems; this sometimes produces big flocks of shearwaters in unexpected places, or it occasionally is responsible for 'wrecking' birds, such as Leach's petrel, far inland. Now and then, seabirds from distant parts of the globe appear in our waters—rare petrels and shearwaters, for example, and even albatrosses from time to time. The magnificent frigatebird from the tropics has turned up, and one black-browed albatross (it is probably the same individual each year) has spent every summer since 1967 with our breeding gannets, first on Bass Rock in the Firth of Forth and, more recently, at Hermaness in Shetland.

Wildfowl

Somewhere, at some time, most wildfowl species—swans, geese and ducks—occur at the coast, usually in estuaries or on coastal marshes where they feed ashore or in shallow water, or seek safe roost-sites or loafing-places. The great majority of them are winter migrants, coming from as far away as Greenland, Iceland, the most northern reaches of Europe and Siberia. Of all the dabbling, surface-feeding duck, wigeon are the most coastal species, grazing on saltmarsh grasses or on the alga *Enteromorpha* in the intertidal zone. Of the various species of diving ducks, goldeneye and scaup are the most closely associated with the coast—in fact, the scaup is almost exclusively a bird of inshore waters and estuaries in winter. These birds feed on molluscs and other marine invertebrates rather than on fish. Broadly similar habits apply to the true seaduck, the scoters, the eider and the long-tailed duck—all birds which dive from the surface—while the red-breasted merganser, another surface diver, has a bill with finely toothed edges and is a fish-eater; it occurs on both fresh and saltwater.

Shelduck are more like geese than ducks, and are essentially estuarine (although they often breed inland), sharing the intertidal zone with the waders where they feed principally on the tiny snail

Hydrobia. All the geese proper are grazing birds for the most part, using grasslands and stubbles (often at the coast); the brent goose is the only truly coastal species in that it feeds largely on the eelgrass *Zostera* and on *Enteromorpha* in the tidal zone.

Waders

Of all the birds which use coastal habitats, it is the waders which show the greatest diversity of form and the greatest ability to exploit almost every conceivable habitat niche. Even the open sea is included: the tiny phalaropes breed around freshwater pools and marshes in the short northern summer, but winter on the open sea, swimming buoyantly and picking up plankton from the surface. Hundreds of thousands of waders use our estuaries in any one year, many of them passing through from the north (where the majority of them breed, often in non-coastal habitats such as tundra, marshes and lakes) and fattening up before pressing on to their wintering grounds further south; many thousands also spend the winter around our shores.

Of the 30 or so species which regularly occur around the coasts of the British Isles (there are at least 20 more rarities from Asia and even North America), many use coastal pools and marshes or the intertidal zone where, according to the lengths of their legs and bills, they can

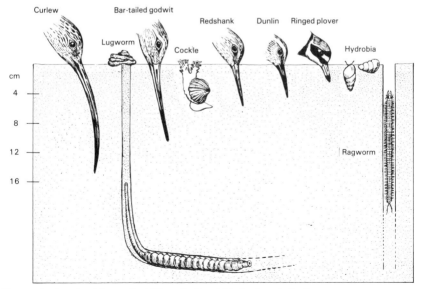

The varying lengths of the waders' bills make it possible for them to feed on different types of shorelife.

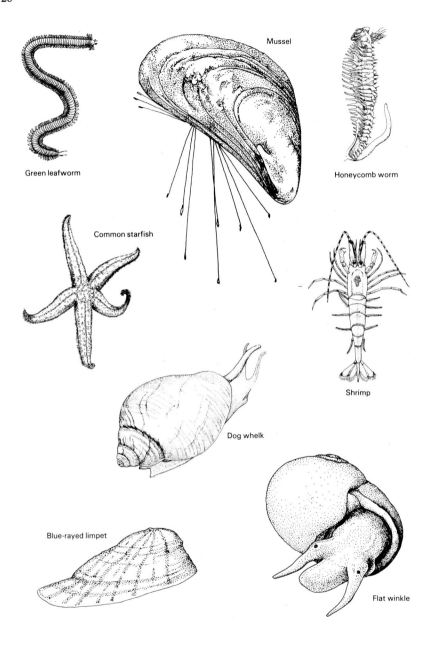

Green leafworm

Mussel

Honeycomb worm

Common starfish

Shrimp

Dog whelk

Blue-rayed limpet

Flat winkle

Some of the shorelife which form the prey of waders and other birds.

utilise a whole range of mini-habitats, from shallow water to open mud. While many of the smaller waders, like dunlin, sanderling and the stints, feed from the surface of the mud or just below it, larger species such as godwits and curlews can probe deeply, finding their hidden prey by touch as well as by visual clues on the surface, and also feed in quite deep water. Oystercatchers have strong, stout bills which enable them to open large shellfish, either on the open shore or in rock pools and among rocks, where the much smaller purple sandpiper tackles the smaller species of shellfish. As their name suggests, turnstones turn over stones and assorted tidal debris in search of food—they are mainly birds of the rockier parts of the shore. Avocets use their curious upturned bills to filter invertebrates from the water itself.

The avocet is distinguished from other waders by its bill which it uses to filter food.

Gulls and Terns

While gulls obviously *do* occur all round our coasts, the name 'seagull' is often a misnomer: only the kittiwake, a thoroughly marine bird, and perhaps the great black-backed gull deserve this title. Many gulls actually nest inland and large numbers are present in all sorts of inland habitats in winter. No doubt there are some gulls which never see the sea at all! Gulls are among the most versatile and successful of all birds, 'all-rounders' which, between them, are able to exploit food supplies from all habitats, including the open sea; they are nimble on land, swim well and are invariably superb fliers. In addition, most are scavengers and, particularly the larger species, active predators of other birds, their eggs and their young. The gulls' ability to adapt to changing circumstances and to co-exist with man has enabled some, like the herring gull, to increase their numbers and distribution enormously, benefiting from rubbish tips and sewage outfalls and even nesting on buildings in cities and towns.

Population explosions among gulls can cause problems for their close relatives, the terns. These are much more specialised and less adaptable birds that take their food (largely fish) from the open water by plunge-diving from the air. Tern colonies are numerous, but often at risk—direct competition for space with man affects the little tern especially. Two species, the Sandwich and the roseate terns, are among the scarcest European breeding seabirds for which we in Britain and Ireland have an international responsibility to conserve and protect.

Skuas and Auks

Gulls may be great scavengers, but the arch-pirates in this respect are the skuas. Two species, pomarine and long-tailed, are passage migrants; another two, the fast-flying, agile Arctic skua and the big, buccaneering bonxie or great skua, breed among the islands of northern Scotland. Both feed and scavenge much as gulls do, but they have also perfected the art of kleptoparasitism—relentlessly chasing, harrying, bullying and even physically assaulting auks, gulls, kittiwakes and terns, and forcing them to drop or disgorge their last catch; bonxies are big enough to tackle even gannets in this way. While the Arctic and great skuas are both northern breeders (in regions rich in other seabirds), they also occur in most other coastal waters in autumn, taking their living from the gulls and terns around low-lying coasts and estuaries.

With the auks, which are in a sense the northern equivalent of the penguins of the Southern Hemisphere, we return to a group of birds which feeds mainly on fish, diving from the surface and swimming strongly underwater, often far from land. With the exception of the black guillemot, they breed in large, frequently immense colonies and either feed just offshore or well out to sea. Competition among them is avoided by their use of different kinds of nest-site and by their different bills, which enable them to catch fish of different kinds and sizes. Alone among them, the tystie or black guillemot is an inshore bird, never venturing far out to sea. The largest of these birds was the great auk, extinct since the mid-nineteenth century after human persecution; it was a flightless, highly specialised fish-eater which lived on remote cliffs and stacks and must have taken much larger prey than the other auks.

We cannot close this brief account without some mention of the other birds associated with coastal habitats, many of which are not, in the strict sense, seabirds or wetland birds. Birds of prey and owls may hunt the shore and saltmarshes, especially in winter, taking wildfowl and waders as well as small landbirds found there—peregrine, merlin, hen harrier and short-eared owl are some of these hunters which come readily to mind. In fact, peregrines and some golden eagles are true members of the coastal community where they breed on sea cliffs and feed mainly on seabirds. The white-tailed eagle, now re-introduced on Rum (Rhum) and hopefully soon to be numbered again among our breeding birds, is a true coastal species in every way.

The list of passerine birds which use coastal habitats in some way or another is a very long one—but many of these are just as common, or more so, in other places. Those which exploit marshes and shores include, for example, crows, starlings, wagtails and pipits, finches and buntings (often in large winter flocks), larks and great grey shrikes. Rock pipits are the only true coastal passerines, but a good case might be made for several others which spend their lives by the sea—notably wrens and skylarks. A few winter visitors are much more closely associated with saltmarshes and deserted beaches than other habitats; shorelarks, snow and Lapland buntings and twites are part of this group which further adds to the diversity of our coastal birdlife.

Birdwatching on the Coast

What do you need to do to be a birdwatcher? The answer is, simply, as much or as little as you choose. It is very much a hobby which can be tailored to suit your own inclinations, spare time and pocket; it can be as strenuous or as relaxing, as serious or as light as you want it to be. The main thing is that it should be enjoyable. It will take you to interesting places and will enable you to meet lots of like-minded people—and, above all, it will be immensely satisfying, both for the genuine pleasure it gives and for leading you towards an under-standing and appreciation of the natural world around you. Since this is a book about birds of the sea and the coast, most of what follows is written with that very much in mind. Most birdwatchers live inland, so we hope that those who are lucky enough to live by the sea will forgive us if we sometimes stress points which, to them, seem rather obvious!

Basic Equipment

A birdwatcher's equipment is important but, in fact, there is not too much of it and, at least in comparison with other hobbies or sports, it need not be too expensive. The 'musts' are, initially, a good pair of binoculars, a notebook and a reasonable selection of reference books; some attention also has to be paid to the right sort of clothing and, later on, serious thought should be given to owning a telescope.

Binoculars and telescopes

Binoculars are very much a matter of personal choice and what you can afford. Some cost a few hundred pounds (not surprisingly, these are generally very good), but it is quite possible to buy a perfectly satisfactory pair for well under £100. There are also many types of cheap Japanese-made binoculars available, all very similar in spite of their many different names, and these should not be ignored: some are very good and sturdy enough to stand years of heavy usage. Don't worry if other people's glasses are bigger, flashier or more expensive-looking than yours—there are always some people who seem to think that there is merit in owning the latest, biggest glasses available, but they are only kidding themselves. Appearances are not important; after all, what you need are binoculars which suit your own require-ments and which work efficiently.

Never buy binoculars by mail-order, and beware of unnecessary gimmickry like zoom lenses, which are hardly worth the bother or the extra expense. There are several makes of binoculars designed for spectacle-wearers; if you need them, ask about these before making your choice. Shop around, looking at what you can afford, and try out as many kinds as you can until you find the pair which suits you best. If you can, seek the advice of other birdwatchers or, better still, get them to go to the shop with you. Be sure, too, to try out the binoculars *outside* the shop!

As for magnification, anything between seven- and ten-times magnification will be fine; many birdwatchers find x 10 good for coastal work, especially since the birds you will want to look at are very often quite far away. More than x 10 is not necessary, and you should avoid being taken in by those occasional advertisements you see for 'fantastic' x 20 and x 25 glasses. You would need the wrists and arms of Superman to use them! For long-distance work, it is really better to invest in a telescope, which is far easier to use once you get accustomed to it. Most modern binoculars give a reasonably wide field of view, which is sometimes worth thinking about in coastal habitats. Broadly speaking, the greater the magnification, the smaller the field of view—but even at x 10 this will be quite adequate.

Light-gathering power is also important. All binoculars carry a legend such as '7 x 50' or '10 x 50'; the first figure indicates the magnification and the second the diameter (in millimetres) of the object lens, the big one furthest from the eye. Divide the second figure by the first, and if your answer comes to four or more, then you can be sure that the light-gathering power of the glasses is suitable. The bigger the answer, the better the glasses are in this respect. Glasses that are 7 x 50 are rather scarce nowadays, but they have exceptional light-gathering qualities which make up for what they might lack in terms of simple magnification; they are particularly good in poor light.

It takes a fair amount of practice to know how 'good' binoculars are in terms of their resolution of detail and how quickly and satisfactorily they can be brought into sharp focus, but by trying out several makes (and several of the same make—there is often a surprising amount of individual variation, particularly with the cheaper types), you will soon see how they compare. A birdwatching friend can be of invaluable help here and another good ploy is to try out a really expensive pair which you can use as a yardstick by which to assess the others. Beware of binoculars which show a rainbow effect round the edges of the 'picture'—these are optically unsatisfactory.

It is important to look after your binoculars and keep them clean—the lenses and moving parts especially—because, above all else, your binoculars are a vital part of your gear. Manufacturer's advice on care and cleaning is often included with your glasses when you buy them.

Telescopes are recommended for use at the coast, where you will often need that extra bit of magnification. There is nothing more frustrating than being unable to make out that diver or seaduck because it is just beyond the range of your binoculars. At first, telescopes are not easy to use; some support is really necessary and, because they need such fine focusing, they have to be held very steady. Cinema-going birdwatchers roll about with laughter when film stars whip 'scopes up to their eyes and immediately announce that they can see all sorts of fantastic detail (this is almost as laughable as the famous 'figure-of-eight' picture we are always shown when our hero is looking through binoculars). A telescope can be rested on anything solid—your car window, a post, a rock and so on. With practice, you will find you can fold up your legs and body into all sorts of impossible positions when you are lying on a beach or a grassy bank, so that you can use your knee as a support. When standing up, a companion's shoulder often proves very useful, too. Nowadays, many bird-watchers own modern, lightweight tripods which are collapsible and highly portable and are designed to take today's modern, lightweight telescopes.

What kind of 'scope should you look for? The older type of many-draw, mainly brass telescopes can still be bought and are often optically superb, despite having a small field of view, but they are usually expensive (especially when repairs are necessary) and fairly heavy. A good deal of practice is also required to use them efficiently. Today, most birdwatchers choose short, lightweight prismatic instruments, of which there are several good makes, and use them with tripods. As with binoculars, decide what you can afford, try out several makes and—most importantly—seek the advice and help of a birdwatcher with good telescope experience. Here, too, you should avoid buying through mail-order.

Notebooks

Most birdwatchers favour notebooks with stiff covers. The water-proof kinds are generally the best, especially those where the edges of the cover overlap the pages. Few things are as annoying as a sodden notebook in which most of what you have laboriously written down is

3rd September.   N. Norfolk coast

Little Gull juvenile / 1st winter.

8×40's. Good light; calm + clear.

Little   Kitt.

Dark nape —
but also
crown
(unlike Kittiwake)

Black outer primaries

Black on rump - rules
out Kittiwake

Black tailband
(tail slightly
notched)

Grey centres? Not so
white as juv Kittiwake

Black band
across coverts

Pale tips?

White streaks show
when feathers spread

Underwing
white

Blackish zigzag / W pattern like young Kittiwake
but dark crown, dark sides of breast, dark
bars across scapulars and dark patch on rump
all unlike Kittiwake — obviously young Little
Gull moulting from juvenile to first winter.
Small, dainty, tern-like but broader-winged.
Tiny black bill. Kittiwakes nearby noticeably
bigger, more powerful action.

A page from a birdwatcher's notebook.

illegible. Many people use loose-leaf notebooks and simply replace the pages, while others buy new notebooks as necessary: it all depends on whether you want to keep your field notebooks as a permanent record of your observations, or whether you 'write up' your notes in a more permanent and detailed form at home.

What you actually put in your notebook is entirely up to you. This can vary from a diary-style treatment, to mere lists of things you have seen, with the date, weather, etc. also recorded; before long, you will probably also want to make notes on behaviour, feeding and so forth, as well as identification features, perhaps with maps, sketches and so on. Develop your own style to suit your own interests: all we would say is that it is our firm belief that no real birdwatcher is ever without a well-used notebook!

Clothing
There is no birdwatcher's 'uniform', although you might, on occasion, be forgiven for thinking otherwise. You can wear more or less what you like, depending on the weather—but a few general tips are given here, based on experience.

At the coast it is often cool, even during what passes for summer in these islands, and in winter it is almost invariably windy and distinctly cold—so bear this in mind and dress accordingly. There is nothing worse than not enjoying a good day's birding because you aren't warm enough, so wear enough sweaters and invest in some warm, windproof trousers—and don't forget to sort out a really good pair of gloves. Thermal underwear or 'winter woollies' should not be spurned, even if you think they might be unfashionable. Most birdwatchers like to have some sort of outdoor jacket or anorak, which should be both warm and at least showerproof and should reach down over your bottom; make sure it has plenty of pockets, too. If it has a hood, so much the better but, if not, a suitable hat does just as well. In many ways, duffle-coats are superb for winter wear at the coast—but, for some reason, they seem to be out of fashion at the moment.

Perhaps the most important thing is to have warm feet in winter. Many of the better kinds of walking boots or stout shoes are fine, worn with heavy socks, but it is worth remembering that, at this time of the year, you are bound to encounter water and mud at some stage, so a good, robust pair of rubber boots are a good bet, worn with heavy socks or modern 'boot liners', of which the best kind are those made of quilted nylon and filled with polyester.

Reference books
We come now to your birdwatching library. The present book will help you name many of the birds you are likely to see, but you will also need a good field guide for identification purposes. In our view, the best is still *A Field Guide to the Birds of Britain and Europe* (Collins) by Peterson, Mountfort and Hollom: this has excellent illustrations and the most complete text of them all. Its only real drawback is that most of the illustrations are far divorced from the appropriate text. This has been overcome in several other guides where the text and the pictures are on facing pages—although, inevitably, the text can be very short and not always complete when this format is adopted. The best guides of this kind are *The Birds of Britain and Europe, with North Africa and the Middle East* (Collins) by Heinzel, Fitter and Parslow, and *The Hamlyn Guide to the Birds of Britain and Europe* by Bruun and Singer. Two other books (which, unlike the foregoing, are purposely designed *not* to fit in your pocket), which use a different system of illustration by showing birds 'in action' rather than just as portraits, are *The Birdlife of Britain* (Mitchell Beazley/RSPB) by Hayman and Burton and *What's That Bird?* (RSPB) by Hayman and Everett. The first of these has also been produced as a scaled-down pocketbook called *The Mitchell Beazley Birdwatcher's Pocket Guide.* Another book we can thoroughly recommend, not least because of its outstandingly good illustrations (probably the best available at the moment), is *Birds of Sea and Coast* (Penguin Nature Guides) by Jonsson. The only field guide dealing specifically with seabirds is *A Field Guide to the Seabirds of Britain and the World* (Collins) by Tuck and Heinzel—although we have to say that the illustrations in this are very disappointing.

There are a number of books giving background information, only a few of which can be mentioned here. *The Seabirds of Britain and Ireland* (Collins) by Cramp, Bourne and Saunders is an invaluable reference work which describes Operation Seafarer—the first attempt, a dozen years ago, to count all our breeding seabirds—and also gives other good background information. Even better, because it covers other species, too, is *The Atlas of Breeding Birds in Britain and Ireland* (Poyser) by Sharrock. Among the many books on wildfowl, we can particularly recommend two by Ogilvie, *Ducks of Britain and Europe* and *Wild Geese* (both published by Poyser). A major work on waders and other coastal birds by Prater, detailing the 'Birds of Estuaries Enquiry', is to be published soon and will be well worth seeking out. *Waders* (Collins New Naturalist Series) by Hale gives excellent background to this fascinating group of shorebirds. For seabirds generally, we can suggest *Seabirds* by Saunders, a Hamlyn paperback, and also *Seabirds: Their Biology and Ecology* (Hamlyn) by Nelson. Finally, a book which we can also thoroughly recommend is *Birdwatching on Estuaries, Coast and Sea* (Severn House Naturalists Library) by Lloyd.

There are dozens of other books on seabirds and coastal species, but we feel that those we have mentioned will be good starters for your ornithological library. Again, the advice of an experienced birdwatching friend will be invaluable in helping you decide which books to buy.

Birdwatching

What about the actual process of birdwatching in coastal habitats? For many people, this will involve making special trips away from home, but the basic rules still apply. Don't be in too much of a hurry to see and identify everything at once. There is no such thing as an 'instant birdwatcher' and you will only become proficient through practice, practice and more practice, eventually getting to know the common shorebirds and seabirds thoroughly. Don't neglect your 'homework'—read your bird books and refer to them constantly; in this way you will learn a great deal and will be surprised at how much of it you can retain in your memory.

Get to know the birds' 'field marks'—check to see if they have white rumps like greenshanks, white wing-bars like many small waders, long or short legs, and so on. Be aware, too, that while there may be little difference in plumage between the sexes in coastal birds, the same is not always true of adults and immatures—gulls are a good case in point. Practise making notes and drawings of, for example, gulls and waders, until you get to know the names of their 'parts' (*see* the drawing on page 39) and their distinguishing features; two common species like black-headed gull and dunlin are good ones on which to start. It is well worth devoting time to this notebook discipline, which is tricky at first but becomes easier with practice. The identification features on many shorebirds and some seabirds are very subtle and you won't remember everything unless you take good notes: then, when that oddity or rarity comes along, your experience with commoner species and your ability to make detailed but concise notes will stand you in good stead.

Shape and movement are every bit as important as plumage details. How does the bird fly, swim or walk? Does it dive from the surface like an auk or a diver, or from the air like a gannet or a tern? Does it fly fast and direct like a seaduck, flutter low over the waves like a storm petrel, or glide on stiff wings, banking this way and that, like a fulmar or a shearwater? Does it run in short spurts like a ringed plover, race along the tideline like a sanderling, or walk with the steady, deliberate gait of a curlew? These and many more things— length of legs, shape of wings and bill and so forth—are immensely important in identifying birds and are all things to learn in the field.

Topography of a bird

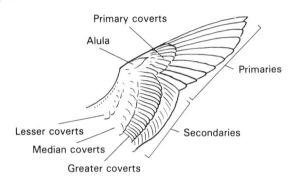

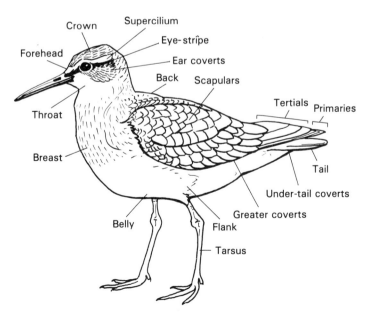

Think, too, about the time of year and the birds' habitats, which in themselves are often important aids to identification. For example, you are unlikely to see a little tern in midwinter, or a long-tailed duck in midsummer; nor are you normally likely to see many small waders around big seacliffs, or puffins on mudflats.

Try not to learn your birds with your binoculars in one hand and your field guide in the other. It really is better to go to the book afterwards, armed with your notes, rather than looking up the birds on the spot. This will make you a much better and more thorough observer—and, in any case, you will undoubtedly come unstuck on that day when you've left the book at home or in the car. Lastly, never be too shy to ask other, more experienced observers to help you. You can learn far more in this way than from books alone, and often a day in the field with a knowledgeable companion is worth ten days on your own.

As a general guide, all the major estuary systems and their associated marshes (and often inland waters close by) are good for waterfowl, shorebirds and, of course, gulls—a group you should not neglect but study closely and learn thoroughly. Most of the 'true' seabirds (fulmars, gannets, shags, kittiwakes, auks, etc.) breed in big colonies in the north and west, often on islands or offshore stacks but also, in some places, on or within easy reach of the mainland, for example, South Stack on Anglesey, Bempton Cliffs, Humberside and St Bees Head, Cumbria. Certain islands, notably Bass Rock in the Firth of Forth and the Farnes off Northumberland, are fairly easy to get to, but others require a major expedition.

Some of the best and most accessible seabird colonies, and many good estuaries and other coastal sites, are nature reserves; all these are shown on the map on page 22 . The various national organisations listed on pages 43–45 will help with information on where to go. Local ornithological societies and clubs, Nature Conservation Trusts and RSPB members' groups are all worth joining for information on where to birdwatch—and, more importantly, to enable you to take part in birdwatching trips, surveys and other organised fieldwork and conservation activities, and to get in touch with other birdwatchers who can help with suggesting the best spots, including those for 'seawatching' from coastal promontories, high cliffs, etc. Don't worry about being a beginner (after all, everybody was once); learn all you can from more experienced people, most of whom are only too willing to help if asked.

One aspect of birdwatching a book cannot cover adequately is birds' voices. While many 'true' seabirds are not very vocal, except at their breeding grounds, many waders and wildfowl (geese especially) can often be identified by voice alone. There are a number of good recordings available on records and tapes which will help you, but there is really no substitute for learning bird calls in the field—slowly and methodically, just as with learning birds by sight. As we have already recommended, go out with experienced birdwatchers and learn from them because, in this field particularly, they are likely to be of more long-term help to you than all the books and recordings in the world!

Fieldcraft is an art all too often neglected by modern birdwatchers. On the coast, you will often be exposed and conspicuous, but make what use you can of any cover available; avoid being on the skyline as far as possible and watch from behind or in front of sea walls, pillboxes, etc. rather than from on top of them. Sit down to watch pools and marshes rather than blundering into and through them and, with nesting birds, observe from a distance whenever you can. Never harass or constantly flush tired migrants and feeding or sleeping birds. Nowadays, on many coastal reserves, good hides offer comfortable shelter as well as camouflage, but when these are not available, look for natural hiding-places among rocks, dunes, breakwaters, etc., and (if safe to do so) use the *insides* of pillboxes. There are also good possibilities for using a car as a mobile hide, which is frequently very handy in bad weather and particularly useful with wary and difficult birds like wild geese.

There are certain important 'do's and don'ts' we must mention. For your own safety, take the utmost care on tidal marshes and mudflats. Find out about the times of tides and safe access routes—being cut off by the tide can be a terrifying (and very uncomfortable) experience, but it can be easily avoided with a little forethought. Steep slopes, banks and, especially, cliffs are *exceedingly dangerous*: do not climb about on them, or attempt to go down them for a better look at the birds. Always be extra careful on grassy slopes above the sea, on wet chalk and loose screes and on rocky areas, especially on wet and windy days. One slip may be the last you will ever make. Boots with a good grip are recommended in rocky sites. If you are in a remote place, especially on an island, remember that communications are difficult and help may be some distance away; whenever possible, leave word as to where you are going, and when you expect to be back. Finally, if you are at sea in a small boat, wear a lifejacket; it may be a nuisance, but it may also save your life.

The welfare of the birds is also important. The golden rule is never to cause disturbance to birds, whether they are on their breeding grounds or in large feeding or roosting flocks. Walk round, not through, colonies of gulls and terns, and avoid putting to flight flocks of roosting or feeding waders and wildfowl. Any breeding bird requires particular care—and it is important to remember that almost all species and their eggs are protected by law. A licence is required even to visit the nests of certain rare species. Full details of the law and its requirements can be obtained from the RSPB in their booklet, *Wild Birds and the Law*. Never trespass, and obey signs regarding access, dangerous cliffs, etc.—they are put there to help you—and always abide by the rules of access or the warden's instructions on nature reserves.

When all is said and done, most birds *can* be watched without causing any problems to them or yourself. All that is needed is common sense and a sensible regard for their welfare—and your own.

Ornithological and Conservation Societies

One of the best ways to find out more about birds and birdwatching is to go out with those who really know. Local trips plus longer excursions to nature reserves and coastal areas are often arranged by your local bird society or group; their address can usually be found at the public library. Another way to learn more is to go away on a course; these are arranged by several societies and their advertisements regularly appear in *Birds* and *Natural World*.

A list of national ornithological societies and other useful addresses follows, together with a short description of what each one has to offer.

Royal Society for the Protection of Birds, The Lodge, Sandy, Bedfordshire SG19 2DL.
Owns or leases over 80 reserves in Britain and Northern Ireland, including some on the coast. Members receive the quarterly magazine, *Birds*, and special reduced rates when visiting reserves; local members' groups in particular areas arrange birdwatching trips, lectures and film shows. The junior section of the RSPB for young people 15 years old and under, the **Young Ornithologists' Club**, organises projects, outings and courses, and members receive a bi-monthly magazine, *Bird Life*.

British Trust for Ornithology, Beech Grove, Tring, Hertfordshire.
A must for birdwatchers who enjoy ornithological field work, the Trust's members join in active field studies, ringing and census work. The BTO always has a number of projects on the go, both organised from headquarters and run by individuals. Its ringing scheme is the most important of its permanent projects and involves co-ordination of the scheme throughout Britain and Ireland and analysis and publication of results. Members receive a six-weekly newsletter, *BTO News*, and a quarterly journal, *Bird Study*. Ringers receive the journal, *Ringing and Migration*, and the *Ringer's Bulletin*.

Royal Society for Nature Conservation, The Green, Nettleham, Lincoln LN2 2NR.
Formerly the Society for the Promotion of Nature Conservation, this

organisation co-ordinates the work of the local Nature Conservation Trusts throughout Britain and Northern Ireland, and covers all aspects of nature conservation. All areas, either a single county or group of counties, have their own individual Trusts and, together with the RSNC, they own or manage 1270 reserves which are usually of local rather than national interest; many of them are open to members. Members join the local Trust (address obtainable by sending a s.a.e. to the RSNC), and receive the magazine, *Natural World*, three times a year, as well as local newsletters.

WATCH, The Green, Nettleham, Lincoln LN2 2NR.
The junior branch of the RSNC organises national projects, as well as outings and activities arranged by local groups. Members receive *WATCHWORD* three times a year.

Wildfowl Trust, Slimbridge, Gloucestershire.
Best known for its wildfowl collections, these are good places to learn duck and goose identification. It also manages wildfowl refuges for ducks and geese and carries out census work and research. Members gain free entry to all the refuges and collections, and receive *Wildfowl* and periodical bulletins.

British Ornithologists' Union, c/o the Zoological Society of London, Regent's Park, London NW1 4RY.
The senior ornithological society in Britain, its object is to promote the scientific study of birds throughout the world. To this end, it publishes a quarterly journal, *Ibis*, and organises conferences. Membership is by election.

International Council for Bird Preservation, 219C Huntingdon Road, Cambridge CB3 0DL.
An organisation which promotes international co-operation in the field of bird conservation, it is especially active in the areas of oil pollution, protection of birds of prey and the trapping of migrant birds. Britain, like most other countries, has its own section of the ICBP.

Seabird Group, c/o British Trust for Ornithology (*see above*).
The Group co-ordinates and funds many amateur studies of seabirds, but is perhaps best known for the national survey, Operation Seafarer. It maintains close liaison with other groups in Africa, Australia and the Pacific. Members receive a newsletter three times a year and the *Seabird Report* biennially.

Irish Wildbird Conservancy, c/o Royal Irish Academy, 19 Dawson Street, Dublin 2.

The Irish equivalent of the British Trust for Ornithology, the IWC also owns and manages a number of reserves including several on the coast. Members receive a regular newsletter.

Irish Wildlife Federation, 8 Westland Row, Dublin 2.

The Irish equivalent of local Nature Conservation Trusts, the Federation arranges lectures for its members and provides educational programmes for teachers and schoolchildren on all aspects of nature conservation. Members receive a newsletter, *Badger.*

Nature Conservancy Council, 19/20 Belgrave Square, London SW1X 8PY.

The British government body for nature conservation, it provides advice and manages the National Nature Reserves.

British Birds, c/o Macmillan Journals Ltd, 4 Little Essex Street, London WC2R 3LF.

A monthly magazine especially for birdwatchers, it includes reports on bird identification, details of sightings of rare birds and up-to-date birdwatching news.

46

Main Coastal Nature Reserves and Bird Observatories

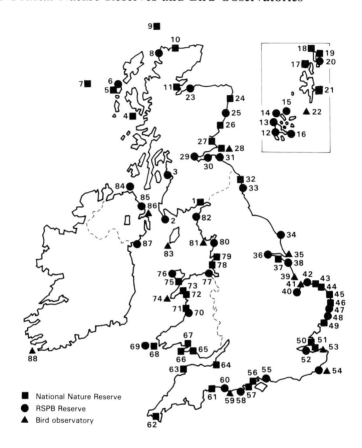

■ National Nature Reserve
● RSPB Reserve
▲ Bird observatory

National Nature Reserves

The Nature Conservancy Council has established 173 National Nature Reserves, some of which are owned or leased by the Council while others are established under nature reserve agreements with the owners.

All its coastal National Nature Reserves are listed here, followed by a number which keys them to the map.

Information on any of these or about the Council itself can be obtained from its Great Britain headquarters; Nature Conservancy Council, 19/20 Belgrave Square, London SW1 8PY. All the reserves have

different regulations and many require permits before entry, so please get in touch with the appropriate regional office before trying to visit them.

Scotland: South-west Region
The Castle, Loch Lomond Park, Balloch, Dunbartonshire G83 8LX.
Caerlaverock (1).
Scotland: North-west Region
Fraser Darling House, 9 Culduthel Road, Inverness IV2 4AG.
Rhum (Rum) (4); Monach Isles (5); St

Kilda (7); North Rona and Sula Sgeir (9); Invernaver (10); Nigg and Udale Bays (11).

Scotland: North-east Region
Wynne-Edwards House, 17 Rubislaw Terrace, Aberdeen AB1 1XE.
Hermaness (17); Haaf Gruney (19); Noss (21); Sands of Forvie (24); St Cyrus (26).

Scotland: South-east Region
12 Hope Terrace, Edinburgh EH9 2AS.
Tentsmuir Point (27); Isle of May (28).

England: North-east Region
Archbold House, Archbold Terrace, Newcastle-upon-Tyne NE2 1EG
Lindisfarne (32).

England: East Midland Region
P.O. Box 6, Godwin House, George Street, Huntingdon, Cambridgeshire PE18 6BU.
Saltfleetby-Theddlethorpe Dunes (37).

England: East Anglia Region
60 Bracondale, Norwich, Norfolk NR1 2BE
Scolt Head Island (43); Holkham (44); Winterton Dunes (45); Walberswick (46); Orfordness/Havergate (49); Leigh (50).

England: South-east Region
'Zealds', Church Street, Wye, Ashford, Kent TN25 5BW.
The Swale (51).

England: South Region
Foxhold House, Thornford Road, Crookham Common, Newbury, Berkshire RG15 8EL.
North Solent (56).

England: South-west Region
Roughmoor, Bishop's Hull, Taunton, Somerset TA1 5AA.
Studland Heath (57); Axmouth/Lyme Regis Undercliffs (61); The Lizard (62); Braunton Burrows (63); Bridgwater Bay (64).

Wales: South Wales Region
44 The Parade, Roath, Cardiff CF2 3AB.
Oxwich (65);
Gower Coast (66);
Whiteford (67).

Wales: Dyfed-Powys Region
Plas Gogerddan, Aberystwyth, Dyfed SY23 3EB.
Skomer (68); Dyfi (71).

Wales: North Wales Region
Plas Penrhos, Ffordd Penrhos, Bangor, Gwynedd LL57 2LQ.
Morfa Dyffryn (72); Morfa Harlech (73); Newborough Warren/Ynys Llanddwyn (75).

England: North-west Region
Blackwell, Bowness-on-Windermere, Windermere, Cumbria LA23 3JR.
Ainsdale Sand Dunes (78); Ribble (79).

RSPB Reserves

The RSPB owns or manages some 80 reserves which cover many types of habitat. Again, the ones listed here are the coastal areas, including mudflats and saltmarsh (which are good for waders) as well as actual seabird colonies.

Many of these reserves can be visited. For full details, write to the RSPB Headquarters, The Lodge, Sandy, Bedfordshire SG19 2DL, enclosing a stamped addressed envelope.

Scotland
Mull of Gallway (2); Horse Island (3); Balranald (6); Handa (8); Hobbister (12); Marwick Head (13); Noup Cliffs (14); North Hill, Papa Westray (15); Copinsay (16); Ramna Stacks (17); Fetlar (20); Nairn Bar, Culbin Sands (23); Fowlsheugh (25); Skinflats (29); Inchmickery (30); Eyebroughty, Fidra and the Lamb (31).

England
Coquet Island (33); Bempton Cliffs (34); Blacktoft Sands (36); Tetney Marshes (38); Snettisham (40); Titchwell (42); Minsmere (47); Havergate Island (48); Elmley Marshes (52); Dungeness (54); Langstone Harbour (55); Arne (58); Radipole Lake (60); Gayton Sands (77); Morecambe Bay (80); St Bees Head (82).

Wales
Grassholm (69); Ynys-hir (70); South Stack Cliffs (76).

Northern Ireland
Rathlin Island Cliffs (84); Swan Island (85); Green and Blockhouse Islands (87).

Bird Observatories

A number of bird observatories, run by independent amateur organisations, have been established around the coasts of the British Isles to study the migration of birds. Birds on passage tend to follow the coasts and stop on islands and headlands to feed or when the weather is bad. The observatories are situated on these places so that the resting birds can be recorded and ringed. Mainly landbirds are studied, but observatories are also excellent places for sea-watching and a number have fine seabird colonies.

Visitors are welcome at observatories; indeed, most of the work carried out is done by them. The observatories usually offer basic accommodation and often run courses in bird-ringing and identification. The best time to visit them is during migration in spring and autumn. Further details on bird observatories can be found in *Bird Observatories in Britain and Ireland,* edited by R. Durman, published by T. & A. Poyser.

Scotland
Fair Isle (22); Isle of May (28).
England
Spurn Point (35); Gibraltar Point (39); Holme (41); Sandwich Bay (53); Dungeness (54); Portland Bill (59); Walney (81).
Wales
Bardsey (74).
Isle of Man
Calf of Man (83).
Northern Ireland
Copeland (86).
Eire
Cape Clear Island (88).

A Selection of Species

The 50 species that have been chosen for this chapter are among those which are most commonly found around the coasts of the British Isles. However, some are rather limited in their distribution, such as the roseate tern and the Slavonian grebe, while others, such as the white-tailed eagle, are extremely rare. These are included because of their interesting history and the fact that their present plight is mainly due to persecution by man or to changes in their environment. The colour photographs and line drawings, together with short notes on identification and way of life of each species, are not intended to be definitive, and reference should be made to field guides for more detailed information.

Much of the information on the 'true' seabirds—gulls, terns, tube-noses, auks—comes from Operation Seafarer, a survey done in 1969/70 when many amateur and professional ornithologists throughout the British Isles, under the auspices of the Seabird Group, worked together to map and count all our seabird colonies. Operation Seafarer was the last major seabird survey but, where possible, these figures have been updated here. Other records on breeding distribution have been gleaned from *The Atlas of Breeding Birds in Britain and Ireland*, published jointly by the British Trust for Ornithology (BTO) and the Irish Wildbird Conservancy (IWC). For this atlas, every ten-kilometre square was visited and checked for presence or absence of breeding species. Information on the winter numbers of waders has been obtained from the 'Birds of Estuaries Enquiry', another survey carried out for four consecutive years and organised by the BTO, RSPB, IWC and the Wildfowl Trust. The participating ornithologists regularly counted the waders found on all the main estuaries of the British Isles. The figures on wintering wildfowl come from the counts organised by the Wildfowl Trust.

To use the maps:

Present breeding distribution

Past breeding distribution

Present wintering distribution

Red-throated Diver

Gavia stellata

Size: 21–27 in (53–69 cm).

Recognition: stream-lined shape, with legs set well back; slender uptilted bill. Red throat only present in breeding season; in winter bird is greyer with white underparts and striking white throat.

Voice: guttural quacking 'kwuck, kwuck, kwuck'; also eerie wail while on water.

Nesting: heap of vegetation by water's edge or on small island. Usually 2 eggs incubated mainly by female for 26–28 days.

Feeding: mainly fish caught underwater; also crustaceans.

Winter plumage

The red-throated diver has a breeding population of about 750 pairs in Britain, but larger numbers winter around the coast. Although protected under Schedule I of the Protection of Birds Acts, unwitting disturbance by human beings is probably the greatest threat to these timid birds. They fly from their nests and it may be an hour or more before they return, during which time the eggs may have chilled or been taken by gulls or crows. They breed mainly in the north and west of Scotland but over the past 90 years they have spread south. They have also increased on the northern and western islands but decreased on the mainland. This decline may be due to fewer numbers of gamekeepers since the war, and hence an increase in foxes and crows which take the eggs.

1890 Breeding area

Slavonian Grebe

Podiceps auritus

Size: 12–15 in (30–39 cm).

Recognition: small, dumpy bird
with straight, stubby bill.
In summer, striking golden tufts
and chestnut flanks and neck;
in winter, black above and white
below.

Voice: penetrating rippling
trill; not very vocal in
winter.

Nesting: floating platform in
sheltered bays of shallow
freshwater lochs. 4–5 eggs;
both sexes share incubation
for up to 25 days.

Feeding: water insects, larvae
and fish obtained by silent
diving; also grasses and water
plants.

Winter plumage

In winter the Slavonian grebes are found round
estuaries and sheltered shores, but they return to
their traditional lochs to breed towards the
end of March. They usually nest in loose
colonies only a few feet apart, or even close
to black-headed gulls. The first nest to be
found in the British Isles was in Inverness in
1908; since then the small population has
slowly built up and there are now about 60
pairs. An annual census of Slavonian
grebes is made and they are
now specially protected under
Schedule I of the Protection of
Birds Acts. Like the red-
throated diver, it suffers from
human disturbance and illegal
egg-collecting. Also very susceptible to rainfall, if the water
is too high or low, its breeding
is affected, and after heavy rain young
are often taken by pike.

Fulmar

Fulmarus glacialis

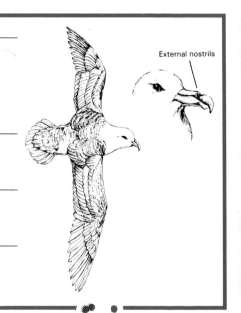

External nostrils

Size: 18–20 in (46–51 cm).

Recognition: heavy head with characteristic external nostrils which relates it to other petrels and shearwaters. Dumpy body, grey above and white below. Flies on stiff wings, wheeling and turning in air.

Voice: series of grunts and crackles when feeding in groups. Succession of guttural notes during display.

Nesting: cliff ledges, old buildings and grassy slopes. 1 egg incubated for 52–53 days by both sexes.

Feeding: crustaceans, squid, fish and offal snatched from water while floating.

The fulmar's story is one of outstanding success. The birds have nested on St Kilda for the past eight or nine centuries, but were not known to breed anywhere else in Britain until 12 pairs were discovered on Foula, Shetland, in 1878. Since then a spectacular increase has occurred, and now almost all suitable nesting cliffs, particularly on the Atlantic coast, are occupied. Various reasons have been suggested for this dramatic increase: the growth of, first, the whaling and, later, the trawling industries that produced large amounts of offal on which fulmars feed; a special genotype which was able to spread south in small colonies; or the warming-up of the north-east Atlantic over the last 100 years. Operation Seafarer estimated the British and Irish fulmar population at about 300 000 pairs, making it one of our most numerous seabirds.

1900 Breeding area

Manx Shearwater

Puffinus puffinus

Size: 12–15 in (30–39 cm).

Recognition: black above and white below; long, slim wings on which it glides close to surface of sea. Only seen on land at night as it shuffles awkwardly to and from its nesting burrow.

Voice: silent by day, but at night eerie screams, gurgles and cackles when near burrow.

Nesting: in close colonies on small islands where both sexes excavate burrow. 1 egg incubated for 51 days by both partners.

Feeding: small fish, squid and crustaceans caught by hovering over surface or shallow diving.

For some time the name 'Manx' shearwater was rather inappropriate as these birds did not breed on the Isle of Man for about 150 years; in 1967, however, they bred once again on the Calf of Man. They have a remarkable homing instinct to their traditional nesting burrows, and in one experiment a shearwater returned from Boston, USA, to Wales in $12\frac{1}{2}$ days. In the past, shearwater chicks have been considered a great delicacy by certain island communities, and this caused a serious reduction in their numbers in some colonies. Accidental introduction of rats to some of their remote island breeding sites has also caused devastation, and in some areas great black-backed gulls are a menace. Colonies are difficult to census but Operation Seafarer estimated that there were at least 175 000 pairs and perhaps over 300 000.

Storm Petrel

Hydrobates pelagicus

Size: 5½–7 in (14–18 cm).

Recognition: tiny blackish-brown bird with white rump and narrow white wing-bar; square-ended tail. Normally seen dancing over sea.

Voice: silent on wing, but at nest an uneven purring noise ending in an abrupt 'hiccough'.

Nesting: in colonies among rocky outcrops, narrow crevices or burrows of other species. 1 egg incubated for about 40 days by both sexes which pair for life. Young leave burrow after about 50 days.

Feeding: mainly small fish, crustaceans and molluscs snatched from surface.

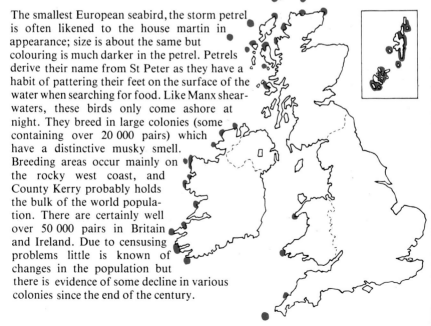

The smallest European seabird, the storm petrel is often likened to the house martin in appearance; size is about the same but colouring is much darker in the petrel. Petrels derive their name from St Peter as they have a habit of pattering their feet on the surface of the water when searching for food. Like Manx shearwaters, these birds only come ashore at night. They breed in large colonies (some containing over 20 000 pairs) which have a distinctive musky smell. Breeding areas occur mainly on the rocky west coast, and County Kerry probably holds the bulk of the world population. There are certainly well over 50 000 pairs in Britain and Ireland. Due to censusing problems little is known of changes in the population but there is evidence of some decline in various colonies since the end of the century.

Leach's Petrel

Oceanodroma leucorrhoa

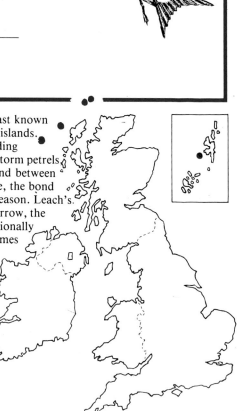

Size: 7½–8½ in (19–22 cm).

Recognition: larger and browner than storm petrel; forked tail that is difficult to see in flight. Springy, darting flight.

Voice: purring, crooning call from within burrow; chattering harsh note varying from guttural to high-pitched on wing over colony.

Nesting: in colonies on isolated offshore islands; usually excavate burrow. 1 egg incubated by both sexes for 41–42 days. Young fledge in 63–70 days.

Feeding: small fish, crustaceans and squid taken while hovering over surface; never dives.

The Leach's petrel is one of our least known seabirds as it nests on such remote islands. The birds arrive back at their breeding areas from April onwards. As with storm petrels they pair for life, but the main bond between the male and female is the nest-hole, the bond being renewed at the start of each season. Leach's petrel prefers to excavate its own burrow, the male digging with its feet and occasionally loosening soil with its bill; sometimes one entrance serves two or more nest-chambers, each a branch off the main tunnel. Breeding is largely restricted to four main island groups in north-west Scotland. Numbers may have increased but it is difficult to tell whether this is a major increase or improved censusing techniques. The total population is probably under 10 000 pairs.

Gannet

Sula bassana

Size: 34–39 in (86–99 cm).

Recognition: our largest seabird; distinct cigar-shaped body, gleaming white with black tips to wings. Juvenile black-brown spangled with white; gradual transition to white over 4 years.

Voice: loud, hoarse 'urrah' on breeding grounds; also croaking call.

Nesting: crowded colonies, usually on cliff ledges but may overflow on to top of cliff. 1 egg incubated beneath webs of feet; both parents share incubation for 44 days.

Food: chiefly fish taken by diving head-first into water.

Adult

Juvenile

The gannet is a magnificent bird to watch, be it flying over the water with regular, rapid wing-beats and glides, or diving spectacularly for food from heights of up to 120 ft (35 m). Its skull is specially adapted to take the impact, its nostrils concealed in the dagger-like bill. Some breeding areas have a long history; the Bass Rock colony (from which the gannet gets its Latin name) was known in the early sixteenth century, and archaeological evidence from the St Kilda colony dates back to the ninth century. During the 1800s, gannets declined in numbers due to persecution by man, but since the beginning of the 1900s, when there were 48 000 pairs, there has been a continual increase. The 16 main colonies around the coast now contain 138 000 pairs, over 70 per cent of the world population.

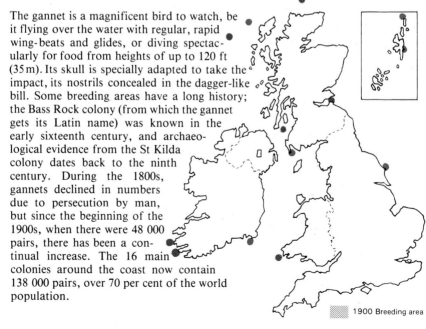

1900 Breeding area

Cormorant

Phalacrocorax carbo

Size: 32–39 in (81–99 cm).

Recognition: large, long-necked bird, browny-black above, bluish-black below. White chin and sides to face, heavy bill; conspicuous white thigh patches in spring. Immature birds have white underparts.

Voice: Low guttural croaking calls at nest-site and roosts.

Nesting: in colonies, on rocky islands, cliff ledges or even in trees. Nest is heap of twigs and seaweed. 3–4 eggs incubated by both partners for 28–31 days. Young fledge in 50 days.

Feeding: fish caught by diving from surface.

Cormorants are often seen inland around lakes and rivers as well as on the coast. Their typical postures are either perching sentinel-like on a post or tree, or with their wings spread out heraldically to dry. Cormorants are sometimes persecuted by man because of their predation of coastal fish, particularly flat-fish, but this is unlikely to have an effect on stocks, and on inland waters the coarse fish on which they prey in turn take young salmon, so they may have a beneficial effect. Surveys show that the species may be declining in north-west Scotland but on the increase in south-east Scotland and Yorkshire. On an island in the Firth of Forth the population increased from 177 to 240 pairs in three years in the 1960s. Operation Seafarer estimated that there were over 8000 pairs in Britain and Ireland.

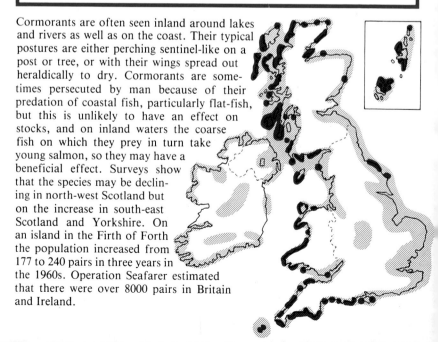

Shag

Phalacrocorax aristotelis

Size: 26–32 in (66–81 cm).

Recognition: smaller, more slender than cormorant with more delicate bill. Close to, plumage is dark, glossy green; crest only present at beginning of breeding season.

Voice: male makes series of croaks; both partners hiss at intruders when on nest, otherwise silent.

Nesting: small colonies in sheltered rocky ledges or caves, particularly at bottom of seacliffs. Nest is heap of vegetation. Normally 3 eggs incubated by both birds for 30–31 days.

Feeding: fish, mainly sand eels, caught underwater.

Winter plumage

The shag is more maritime than the cormorant and is seldom seen far from the coast. These birds dive for fish, rarely taking commercial species, and often stay submerged for about one minute; in clear water they can be watched swimming gracefully underwater. They mainly occur on the west and north coasts and numbers appear to have been increasing, especially on the east coast, since the 1920s. As this coincides with other seabird populations, it is probably caused by climatic changes improving the food supply. Local populations can be dramatically reduced by natural causes. The Farne Island colony was reduced by one-fifth in 1968 by a red tide—an outbreak of poisonous dinoflagellates—but the numbers have since built up. When surveyed for Operation Seafarer, 30 000 pairs were counted, with over three-quarters in Scotland.

68

Brent Goose

Branta bernicla

Size: 22–24 in (56–61 cm).

Recognition: small, stocky goose, black or dark grey above, with white rump which is very obvious in flight. Juveniles lack small white patches on neck.

Voice: shrill, croaking call 'kee-kwa' uttered in flight and by feeding flocks.

Nesting: breeds further north than any other goose. Colonial with shallow nest. 3–5 eggs incubated by female for 24–26 days. Young leave nest soon after hatching.

Food: on wintering grounds, mainly eelgrass (*Zostera*), also other marine plants and algae.

Dark-bellied

Pale-bellied

The brent goose is the most maritime of all geese and is well adapted to life at sea, often seen flying in loose flocks over the waves. They arrive in Britain in October or November, having migrated from their Arctic breeding grounds. There are two main races of brent goose: the dark-bellied *Branta bernicla bernicla* which breeds in Siberia and winters mainly around the east coast of Britain; and the light-bellied *Branta bernicla hrota* from Greenland and northern Canada which migrates mainly to Ireland with small numbers on the north-east coast of Britain. Because these geese nest in the high Arctic, breeding success varies greatly, depending on weather, but after a series of good seasons, the European population of dark-bellied is about 167 000 birds, with counts in Ireland of the light-bellied race of about 16 000.

pale-bellied brents

dark-bellied brents

Shelduck

Tadorna tadorna

Size: 24 in (61 cm).

Recognition: large, rather goose-like bird; very striking plumage of white with bands of dark green, chestnut and black. Female lacks conspicuous knob at base of bill.

Voice: not very vocal; duck croaking 'ark, ark'; drake making soft whistle in courtship.

Nesting: in burrows round sheltered coasts and estuaries. About 8 eggs incubated by duck for 29–31 days.

Feeding: mainly invertebrates— molluscs, insects and crustaceans— obtained by scything action across surface of moist mud or sand.

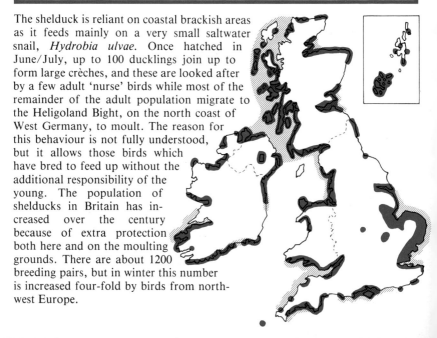

The shelduck is reliant on coastal brackish areas as it feeds mainly on a very small saltwater snail, *Hydrobia ulvae*. Once hatched in June/July, up to 100 ducklings join up to form large crèches, and these are looked after by a few adult 'nurse' birds while most of the remainder of the adult population migrate to the Heligoland Bight, on the north coast of West Germany, to moult. The reason for this behaviour is not fully understood, but it allows those birds which have bred to feed up without the additional responsibility of the young. The population of shelducks in Britain has increased over the century because of extra protection both here and on the moulting grounds. There are about 1200 breeding pairs, but in winter this number is increased four-fold by birds from north-west Europe.

Scaup

Aythya marila

Size: 19 in (48 cm).

Recognition: broad-bodied diving
duck; drake has black head and neck
with white flanks and grey back;
duck is dark brown with white
patch behind bill. Both have
bluish-grey bills.

Voice: duck makes loud, coarse 'krr';
drake is more musical, with dove-like
'wa-hoo' used in display.

Nesting: breeds in Iceland,
northern Europe and Siberia.
8–11 eggs in shallow, grass-
lined cup, incubated for 26–
28 days by duck. Young leave
nest soon after hatching.

Feeding: mainly molluscs—mussels,
cockles and periwinkles; also
seeds and vegetable matter.

Although one or two have been occasionally
reported breeding in northern Scotland, the
scaup is mainly a winter visitor to the British
Isles. They arrive in mid-September to mid-
November and concentrate in bays and
mouths of estuaries. Until recently, huge flocks
of up to 30 000 gathered in the Firth of Forth
where they were attracted to rich feeding
conditions around Edinburgh's sewage
outfalls. Islay is another such site where
the birds feed almost entirely on
waste grain from distilleries.
However, scaup are diving
duck and go down to depths
of 20 ft (6 m) in search of invertebrates living on the sea
bottom. The total number of
birds in north-west Europe is
estimated to be more than
150 000 individuals, but their habit of
congregating in large flocks makes them
very susceptible to oil spills.

Eider

Somateria mollissima

Size: 23 in (58 cm).

Recognition: wide-bodied duck with short neck and long head shaped like a Roman nose. Drake is white above and black below with black cap; female is muted brown all over.

Voice: male makes a variety of coo-ing calls during display; duck has more throaty, cawing call, also harsh 'kuk-kuk-kuk' when danger threatens.

Nesting: mossy hollow on ground, preferably on coastal islands. 4–6 eggs incubated for 25–28 days by duck. Young leave nest soon after hatching.

Feeding: mainly molluscs; also crustaceans and echinoderms.

♀

The eider is well known for giving its name to that cosy article of bedding. In Iceland, down is harvested on eider farms where the birds are encouraged to nest in specially prepared stone hollows. The duck plucks the down from her breast to line the nest and it is usually collected after the young have hatched. The brown-coloured ducklings' journey to the sea is a hazardous one, as many are taken by waiting gulls and skuas. Once at sea they mix with other broods and are looked after in a crèche by several non-breeding or unsuccessful females. The most numerous seaduck in the world with probably more than 2 million in Europe alone, their numbers have been steadily increasing since the mid-1800s, and they are now the second-most numerous duck in Britain and Ireland.

Long-tailed Duck

Clangula hyemalis

Size: 17 in (43 cm); male's tail feathers may add 5 in (13 cm).

Recognition: small, neat bird; male is predominantly white with dark brown patches and long tail streamers; female lacks long tail and is browner on back.

Voice: drake, on water or in air, has beautiful melodious yodelling; duck is less musical and more penetrating.

Nesting: breeds in high Arctic regions on islands and skerries off main coast. Nest is lined depression on ground. 6–9 eggs incubated for 24–29 days by female.

Feeding: crustaceans and molluscs.

♀

Winter plumage

The long-tailed duck is a winter visitor to Britain, arriving in October and leaving in spring. It is found in largest numbers on the north-east coast of Scotland where the drake is usually seen in only one of his three distinct annual plumages. Unique among ducks, the male moults three times: in April, he becomes brown on the back with tail streamers; after breeding in July he moults again to eclipse plumage; and three months later changes into winter dress. The duck is also exceptional: she is the only duck in the northern hemisphere with different summer and winter plumages.

These birds have suffered large losses due to man's activities, from being caught in fishing nets to oil pollution.

There appears to have been a drastic drop in the European population in recent years, estimated at only half a million birds.

Goldeneye

Bucephala clangula

Size: 18 in (46 cm); male larger than female.

Recognition: medium-sized duck, with high crown giving head triangular appearance. Drake is black above, with white neck and underparts; duck has chocolate-brown head with mottled grey-brown back.

Voice: usually silent except in display when male gives series of cheeping and purring calls.

Nesting: in hollows in trees and readily uses nest-boxes. 8–11 eggs incubated for 29–30 days by female. Young drop from nest soon after hatching.

Feeding: molluscs, crustaceans, fish and insect larvae.

♂

The goldeneye is mainly a winter visitor to the British Isles, breeding around the lakes and rivers in the forests of northern Europe and Russia. A few pairs have nested in north Scotland since 1970 and numbers have increased with the provision of nest-boxes in suitable areas. The goldeneye is well known for its display which can be seen in the spring before it leaves for its northern breeding grounds, the male throwing his head back along his back with bill vertical or stretching forward, and splashing water into the air with his feet. Although goldeneye occur in small numbers on lakes and reservoirs, the majority of the established British wintering population of 10–12 000 occurs around the coast. The population appears to be stable and, as the birds stay inshore, they are less susceptible to oil pollution than the long-tailed ducks and scoters.

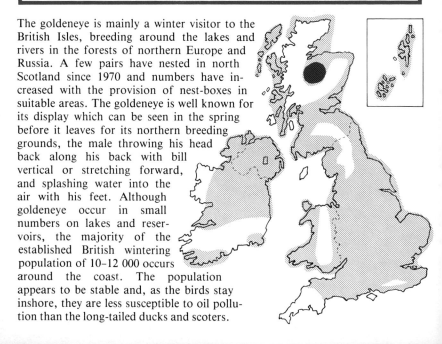

Common Scoter

Melanitta nigra

Size: 19 in (48 cm).

Recognition: male is all black duck with orange-yellow patch on bill; female is brown with pale patch on side of face.

Voice: drake makes musical whistling or hooting notes; duck has more grating, coarser note.

Nesting: lined hollow on ground, well concealed in thick vegetation. 6–8 eggs incubated by female for 30–31 days. Young leave nest soon after hatching and fledge in 45–50 days.

Feeding: mainly mussels obtained by diving; in summer, water plants, insects larvae and crustaceans.

♀

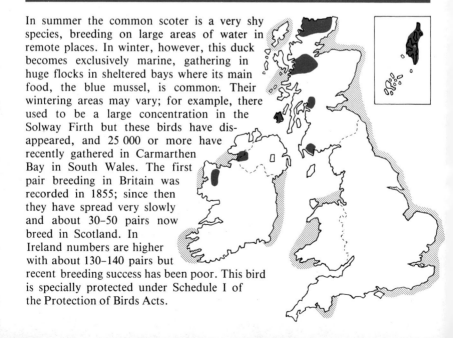

In summer the common scoter is a very shy species, breeding on large areas of water in remote places. In winter, however, this duck becomes exclusively marine, gathering in huge flocks in sheltered bays where its main food, the blue mussel, is common. Their wintering areas may vary; for example, there used to be a large concentration in the Solway Firth but these birds have disappeared, and 25 000 or more have recently gathered in Carmarthen Bay in South Wales. The first pair breeding in Britain was recorded in 1855; since then they have spread very slowly and about 30–50 pairs now breed in Scotland. In Ireland numbers are higher with about 130–140 pairs but recent breeding success has been poor. This bird is specially protected under Schedule I of the Protection of Birds Acts.

Velvet Scoter

Melanitta fusca

Size: 22 in (56 cm).

Recognition: dark duck with white wing-patches conspicuous in flight. On water slightly larger than common scoter; has orange bill and small white area under eye.

Voice: rarely calls; thin whistle during courtship display.

Nesting: breeds around wooded lakes and mountainous areas of northern Europe and Russia. Shallow, lined cup on ground, 7–9 eggs incubated for 27–28 days by female. Young leave nest soon after hatching.

Feeding: mainly molluscs, obtained by diving from surface, particularly dog whelks and periwinkles.

Unlike the common scoter, the velvet scoter is only a winter visitor to our coasts. It is less concerned about rough weather than the other scoters, but even so it frequents sheltered estuaries and bays. A good diver, it regularly feeds at depths of 35–65 ft (10–20 m) for marine snails such as dog whelk (*Nassa* spp) and periwinkles; mussels are also taken. When reared near the coast, the breeding success of the velvet scoter is often very poor; as many as 80–100 per cent of the young are killed by rough storms. The success of the species must depend on the inland breeders. This bird is the least abundant of the European seaducks, and it is seriously threatened by oil-spills. Over 1000 winter around the coast of Britain, and wintering counts in the Baltic number around 30 000.

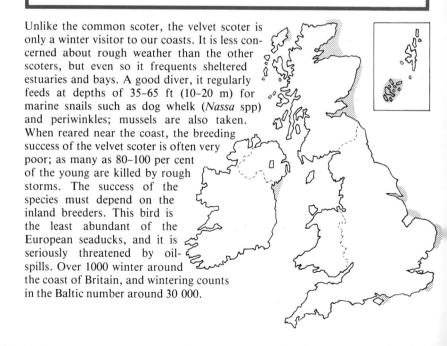

Red-breasted Merganser

Mergus serrator

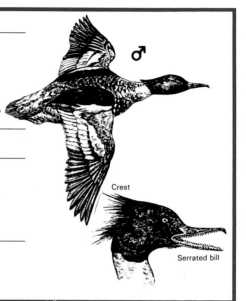

Size: 23 in (58 cm).

Recognition: rather rakish looking with wispy crest and long, thin bill. Dark green head, white collar and dark breast distinct in male. Female has reddish-brown head, mottled grey body.

Voice: male rarely calls; female makes harsh 'kar-r-r'.

Breeding: shallow hollow in long vegetation on ground; occasionally use rabbit burrows. 8–10 eggs incubated by duck for 31–32 days. Young leave nest soon after hatching.

Feeding: primarily fish caught by diving from surface.

Crest

Serrated bill

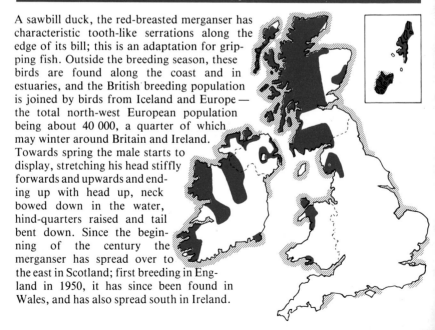

A sawbill duck, the red-breasted merganser has characteristic tooth-like serrations along the edge of its bill; this is an adaptation for gripping fish. Outside the breeding season, these birds are found along the coast and in estuaries, and the British breeding population is joined by birds from Iceland and Europe — the total north-west European population being about 40 000, a quarter of which may winter around Britain and Ireland. Towards spring the male starts to display, stretching his head stiffly forwards and upwards and ending up with head up, neck bowed down in the water, hind-quarters raised and tail bent down. Since the beginning of the century the merganser has spread over to the east in Scotland; first breeding in England in 1950, it has since been found in Wales, and has also spread south in Ireland.

White-tailed Eagle

Haliaeetus albicilla

Size: 27–36 in (69–91 cm);
female larger than male.

Recognition: large vulture-like
eagle, with huge deep bill; female
up to 15 per cent larger
than male. Medium brown all
over with white tail; immatures
have dark tail. In flight very wide,
deeply fingered wings and short,
wedge-shaped tail.

Voice: yelping sound; female
deeper voiced than male.

Nesting: seacliffs or trees near
coast. Nest is huge structure of
branches and twigs. Usually 2
eggs incubated mainly by female
for 38 days.

Feeding: fish, waterbirds, mammals
and carrion.

The white-tailed eagle had occurred in most counties of Scotland and coastal Ireland, north-west England and in Devon and the Isle of Wight, but last bred on Skye in 1916, after which it became extinct in Britain. This was mainly due to human persecution with birds being shot and eggs collected. Attempts have been and are still being made to re-introduce this bird. The first attempt on Fair Isle was unsuccessful as fulmars spat oil over the young eagles as they tried to take their chicks. For the last six years, an extensive programme has been carried out on the island of Rum (Rhum). 37 birds have been released and 25 still survive. Breeding has not yet been recorded as white-tailed eagles do not nest until they are five or six years old, but pairs have been seen holding territories in suitable habitats.

c.1900

* Re-introductions

Oystercatcher

Haematopus ostralegus

Size: 17 in (43 cm).

Recognition: pied bird with bright orange bill and flesh-pink legs. In flight, white below with striking black and white wings and tail.

Voice: loud, shrill 'klee-eep, klee-eep'; in breeding season becomes more of a piping trill.

Nesting: shallow depression on shingle or vegetation mainly near coast. Usually 3 eggs incubated by female for 24–27 days. Young leave nest soon after hatching.

Feeding: mainly molluscs, such as mussels, cockles and limpets; also crustaceans and insect larvae.

Oystercatchers have two methods of opening mussels or cockles. They either hammer the shell open at its weakest point with their powerful bill, or cut the muscle which closes the shell while the bivalve is open. The bird's diet of cockles is said to have economic repercussions, and in South Wales in the 1970s several thousand birds were shot, despite strong protests from conservationists. In winter British birds are joined by those from northern Europe, the population then numbering over 220 000. Since the 1940s there has been a marked increase in the breeding population to about 30 000 pairs, partly due to birds moving inland to nest, first up rivers in the north, then out into the surrounding fields in the valleys and along the coast. Inland nesting has now spread to the south of Britain where gravel pits are also used.

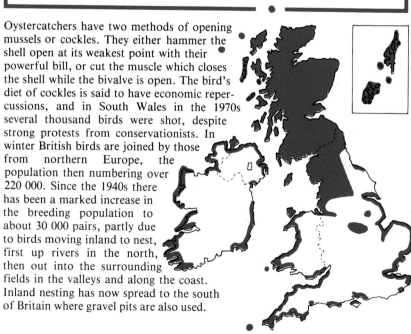

Ringed Plover

Charadrius hiaticula

Size: 7½ in (19 cm).

Recognition: small, dumpy bird with prominent black collar and black and white banding above bill; browny grey above, white below; orange legs. In flight well-marked narrow wing-bar and white sides to tail; similar little ringed plover lacks wing-bar.

Voice: trilling song March to July; melodious 'tooi' when disturbed.

Nesting: hollow in sand or pebbles on beach or inland. Usually 4 eggs incubated by both birds for 24 to 25 days. Young leave nest soon after hatching.

Food: molluscs, insects and worms; some vegetable matter.

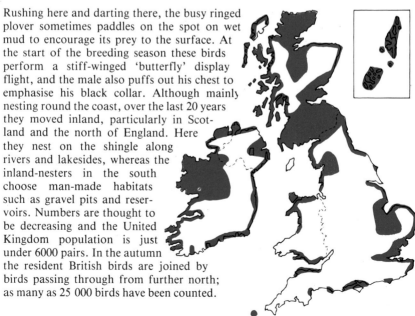

Rushing here and darting there, the busy ringed plover sometimes paddles on the spot on wet mud to encourage its prey to the surface. At the start of the breeding season these birds perform a stiff-winged 'butterfly' display flight, and the male also puffs out his chest to emphasise his black collar. Although mainly nesting round the coast, over the last 20 years they moved inland, particularly in Scotland and the north of England. Here they nest on the shingle along rivers and lakesides, whereas the inland-nesters in the south choose man-made habitats such as gravel pits and reservoirs. Numbers are thought to be decreasing and the United Kingdom population is just under 6000 pairs. In the autumn the resident British birds are joined by birds passing through from further north; as many as 25 000 birds have been counted.

Grey Plover

Pluvialis squatarola

Size: 11 in (28 cm).

Recognition: medium-sized, dumpy wader. In winter fairly uniform greyish brown plumage; black patches under wings in flight. Breeding plumage of striking black belly and face, with silver-spangled grey back.

Voice: three-syllabled 'thee-oo-ee' given in flight.

Nesting: breeds in Arctic tundra of Russia, Siberia and America. Nest is shallow scrape in moss or peat. 4 eggs incubated by both partners for 23 days.

Feeding: wide variety of molluscs, worms, crustaceans and insects; also some vegetable matter.

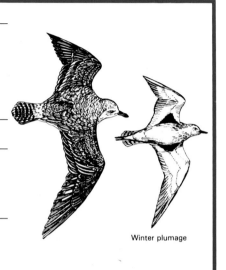

Winter plumage

The grey plover is mainly a winter visitor and passage migrant to the shores of Great Britain and Ireland. It arrives from mid-July to mid-November, departing in mid-March to early June. This bird is unusual in that it often interrupts its moult, migrating down to west Africa with both new and old feathers in its wings. This was discovered when birds on passage, caught on the Wash in eastern England, were found not to be far enough into their moult to complete it before journeying on to their winter quarters; other birds were found to be already in suspended moult. The reasons for this behaviour are not understood, as other species breeding just as far north have time to moult completely on the Wash before starting the final leg of their journey. Coastal mudflats are the main habitat of the grey plover, and about 13 000 winter around the main estuaries.

Turnstone

Arenaria interpres

Size: 9 in (23 cm).

Recognition: stocky bird with mottled back of black, brown and white, often with traces of chestnut summer plumage; white underparts. In flight distinctly pied, but much smaller than oystercatcher.

Voice: twittering, metallic 'kitititit' when flushed.

Nesting: breeds in Scandinavia, Russia and north-east Greenland. Nest is hollow on ground lined with grass and leaves. Usually 4 eggs incubated mainly by female for 22 days.

Feeding: very varied—mainly crustaceans, also molluscs, worms and carrion.

Winter plumage

Winter visitors and passage migrants to our coasts preferring rocky or shingle beaches, turnstones do not breed unil they are two years old and non-breeding birds are often present throughout the summer. As its name suggests, the turnstone uses its short, conical bill to flick over stones and seaweed, picking up the invertebrates from beneath. These provide a rich source of nutrients and birds caught consecutively in Iceland just before migration put on $\frac{1}{2}$ oz (12–15 g) per day. The turnstones which breed in northern Scandinavia pay only a brief visit to our shores, feeding up and moulting, then continuing south to winter in Iberia and west Africa. More northerly breeding birds from Arctic Canada and Greenland arrive slightly later and remain throughout the winter. Birds on the main estuaries number about 9000 but the total population is much larger.

Purple Sandpiper

Calidris maritima

Size: 8 in (20 cm)

Recognition: dark, dumpy bird with sooty upperparts faintly speckled with purple; paler below. Narrow white wing-bar in flight; under-pattern rarely seen as flies low over rocks.

Voice: rather silent in winter, occasional low 'weet-wit', or high twitter in flocks.

Nesting: on coasts of Iceland and Norway. Nests are very hard to find; neat cup with 4 eggs. Incubation chiefly by male, although female takes some part, for 21 to 22 days. Male in sole charge of brood once hatched; fledge in about 3 weeks.

Feeding: mainly molluscs; also small fish, insects and crustaceans.

Like the turnstone, the purple sandpiper is a winter visitor and passage migrant to the coasts of Britain; it too favours rocky shores. It is the least shy of our waders and can often be watched at very close quarters as it scurries around at the base of piers and breakwaters. At a distance, it is difficult to spot, beautifully camouflaged against the boulders, only occasionally taking to the air, then darting behind the next cluster of rocks. On its wintering ground its fairly long bill is used for taking winkles, dog whelks and shore crabs. It feeds near the edge of the water, moving up and down the beach with the tide. It mainly winters in Scotland and on the west coast; birds which are passing through to winter further south occur down the east and west coasts.

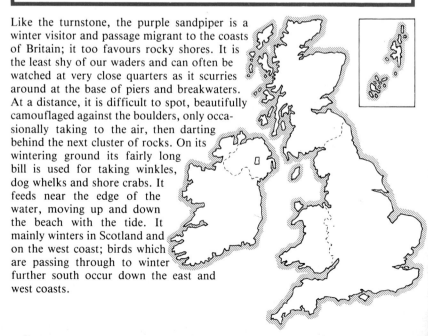

Dunlin

Calidris alpina

Winter plumage

Breeding plumage

Size: 7–8 in (18–20 cm).

Recognition: small wader mainly seen in large flocks; grey above and white below, with narrow white wing-bar. In summer chestnut backed, with black patch on belly.

Voice: rich trill on breeding grounds; ordinary note is a rather nasal 'dzee' when flushed.

Nesting: coastal marshes and inland on upland moors. Nest is neat cup in grass tussock. 4 eggs incubated by both birds for 21 to 22 days. Young fledge in 20 days but may be left by parents earlier.

Feeding: insects, molluscs, crustaceans and worms, probed for in mud or sand.

The dunlin is the commonest of our waders, occurring in huge winter flocks which wheel and turn, flickering grey and white. They feed with bustling activity and studies have shown that fat laid down in the first part of the winter is an insurance against cold weather; once mid-winter has passed their reserves decrease. On the main estuaries in Britain, dunlin numbers reach a peak in January when counts of over 600 000 have been made. Their typical breeding habitat in Britain is damp moorland, whereas in Ireland dunlin choose rough lowland grass near lakes and marshes. These populations are on the extreme south-west of the species range and those on Dartmoor are the most southerly group in the world. Numbers appear to have declined this century; the total breeding in the United Kingdom is about 4000 to 8000 pairs.

Knot

Calidris canutus

Size: 10 in (25 cm).

Recognition: medium-sized, stocky wader, greyish back with white underparts; paler than dunlin. Short, straight, black bill and short legs. In flight has overall grey appearance, often seen in huge flocks of several thousand birds.

Voice: two main calls—hoarse, low-pitched 'knut' and more mellow 'wit wit'.

Nesting: in high Arctic of Canada, Greenland and Siberia. Nest is hollow on ground lined with lichens. 4 eggs incubated for about 22 days by both sexes. Male tends young when hatched.

Feeding: on wintering area, crustaceans, molluscs, worms and insects.

Winter plumage

Both the Latin and common names of the knot are said to be derived from King Knut (Canute) as it often emulates the King in daring the advancing tide. It is a passage migrant or winter visitor to the coasts of Britain and Ireland. Those passing through go south to Patagonia, South Africa and as far as Macquarie Island, but the majority of the world population winters around the coasts of Britain and Ireland with counts on the main estuaries approaching 300 000 birds. On favoured estuaries, such as the Ribble and the Wash, the birds pack so tightly together they they appear almost like a mass of grey mud. In autumn, the more speckled birds are the young of that season, while in spring those with chestnut tinges to their breasts are breeding birds just starting to moult into full summer dress.

Sanderling

Calidris alba

Size: 8 in (20 cm).

Recognition: small, silvery grey wader; short, dark bill and dark shoulder patches. In flight, distinguished from dunlin by striking white wing-bar and very white appearance in winter.

Voice: liquid 'twick twick' in flight or when flushed.

Nesting: on tundra of Canada, Greenland and Siberia. Nest is small scrape lined with leaves. 4 eggs incubated for 24 days mainly by female. Young leave nest soon after hatching and are tended by one parent.

Feeding: on wintering grounds, crustaceans, worms and molluscs; also some vegetable matter.

Sanderling only spend about two months on their Arctic breeding grounds and the female may lay two clutches, incubating one herself and leaving the other to her partner. They then span the globe to winter on the coasts of Britain and Ireland and other parts of northern Europe, South America, the Falkland Islands, southern Africa, New Zealand and Australia. It is thought that only the Greenland breeders make the very long migrations, the Siberian birds wintering on European coasts. Numbers around the British coasts are greatest in the autumn and spring when wintering birds are joined by passage migrants: the autumn peak on British estuaries is about 23 000, with a spring peak of about 27 000. Migration requires extra energy supplies and sanderling can double their weight before moving north, then fly non-stop to their breeding grounds.

Redshank

Tringa totanus

Size: 11 in (28 cm).

Recognition: common, medium-sized wader. Grey-brown back with pale underparts; long red legs and bill with darker tip. In flight, conspicuous, white triangular-shaped rump-patch, white trailing edges to wings.

Voice: penetrating alarm call, either single 'tew' or triple 'tew tew tew'; yodelling song.

Nesting: in damp marshland and grassy fields. Well-concealed nest with 4 eggs. Incubation by both partners for 23 to 24 days. Young leave nest soon after hatching.

Feeding: in winter, mainly crustaceans; when breeding, worms and leatherjackets.

The redshank is often called the 'sentinel of the marshes', as its hysterical alarm call is normally heard before the bird is spotted. At the beginning of the 1800s there was a huge decrease, probably due to drainage, and for the next 50 years the bird was restricted to the counties and islands bordering the North Sea. Since then there has been a gradual spread but nesting birds are now more common in the north than in the south. The current breeding population is thought to be about 50 000 pairs. By about July, the birds desert their inland nesting grounds and move to the coast to join other birds which have nested further north in Europe and are wintering here or just passing through. Counts of over 100 000 have occurred on the main estuaries in September.

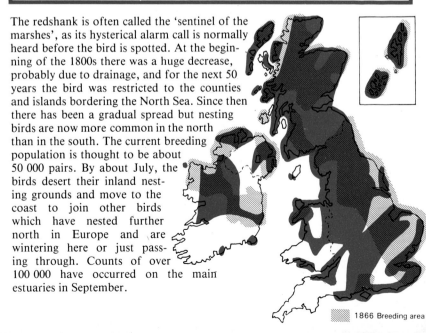

1866 Breeding area

Bar-tailed Godwit

Limosa lapponica

Size: 14–15½ in (36–39 cm).

Recognition: large wader; long, slightly upturned bill and long legs. In flight, brownish with white 'V' on back. Larger black-tailed godwit easily recognised in flight by white wing-bar, black band to tail and long trailing legs.

Voice: rather silent except on breeding grounds; in flight occasional low 'kirric'.

Nesting: on open tundra of northern Scandinavia and Russia, usually on small hummock. 4 eggs incubated mainly by male for about 21 days. Young fledge in about 3 weeks.

Feeding: bivalves and worms; also recently hatched fish and insects.

Black-tailed godwit

The long bill of the bar-tailed godwit is ideal for probing deep into mud for small molluscs or lugworms. These birds prefer to keep to firm, rather sandy mud well away from the tideline, unlike the black-tailed godwit which often wades out into deep water. Bar-tailed godwits do congregate with other waders but more often form large flocks of their own species and perform communal display on the wing—plunging down through the air in wild, twisting dives, uttering their wheezing call rather like geese. They are winter visitors and passage migrants to the coasts of Britain and Ireland, arriving in August and September; about 40 000 over-winter on the main British estuaries. They leave in about February to March for the Waddenzee, off the north-west coast of Germany and Denmark, where they fatten up before moving further north to breed.

Curlew

Numenius arquata

Size: 19–25 in (48–63 cm).

Recognition: largest wader; speckled brown with long, down-curved bill. Female's bill up to one-third longer than male's. Slow leisurely flight, much barring on underwing with darkish neck and breast.

Voice: musical 'coor-lee' call in flight; on breeding grounds, bubbling song as they glide downwards.

Nesting: rough damp pasture and upland moors. Nest is deep scrape lined with grasses. Usually 4 eggs incubated mainly by female for 29–30 days. Young tended by both parents at early stage, later by male.

Feeding: in winter, ragworms and bivalve molluscs; when inland, insects, slugs, snails, berries and seeds.

On muddy estuarine shores the curlew hunts by both touch and sight, probing deep with its sensitive bill or finding its prey by surface clues such as holes or tracks. It winters on the coast from September to February when the main British estuaries hold about 50 000 birds. Most curlews pair before arrival on the nesting area and the territories are probably held by the same pair each year. This century the curlew has spread dramatically, particularly into the lowlands including cultivated farmland, and it breeds in almost every county in Britain and Ireland. Curlews are most common in areas of north Ireland, where rough grassy fields with damp feeding meadows close by provide the ideal habitat. Their expansion seems to have slowed down, but this could still be the effects of the very cold winter of 1962/63 which decreased their numbers considerably.

Whimbrel

Numenius phaeopus

Size: 15–16 in (38–41 cm).

Recognition: plumage and bill very similar to curlew; smaller in size with two distinct dark bands over crown, also slightly darker on back. In flight faster wing-beats than curlew.

Voice: series of tittering whistles in descending pitch, usually 7 in number.

Nesting: far north on bare tundra or dry moorland. Nest is simple scrape. 4 eggs incubated by both sexes for 27 to 28 days. Young tended by both birds until they fledge in about 4 weeks.

Feeding: molluscs, worms, crabs; when inland, insects and berries.

The whimbrel is often regarded as the northern replacement for the curlew, breeding further north and at higher altitudes. In Britain, small numbers breed in north Scotland, particularly Shetland. There was a decline at the end of the last century until the 1930s; the amelioration of the weather was thought to be the cause. Recently, with cooler springs and summers, numbers have improved: since the 1950s they have actually trebled in Shetland. The breeding population of under 200 pairs is now specially protected under Schedule I of the Protection of Birds Acts. It is mainly as a passage migrant that the whimbrel occurs on the coasts of Britain and Ireland, stopping on its journey either to or from its breeding grounds. Usually more numerous in the spring than in the autumn, about 3000 birds are present on the main estuaries in May.

Avocet

Recurvirostra avosetta

Size: 17 in (43 cm).

Recognition: unmistakable black and white wader with long, slender, upturned bill. In flight, rather rounded wings with conspicuous black wing-tips and black-and-white back patterning.

Voice: clear 'kluut' call when disturbed.

Nesting: on islands in brackish lagoons, usually in colonies. Nest varies from simple scrape to elaborate platform. 4 eggs incubated for 22 to 24 days by both sexes. Young tended by both partners and fledge at about 6 weeks.

Feeding: small worms and crustaceans filtered from water with scything action.

The avocet is a conservation success story and credit for its re-establishment as a British breeding bird goes to the RSPB which uses the bird as its emblem. It was extinct as a breeding species in the early nineteenth century. The reason for this is uncertain but both the birds and their eggs were harvested for food. It was nearly 100 years before the avocet bred again; first in County Wexford in 1938, and later, in 1947, breeding was confirmed at both Minsmere and Havergate Island in Suffolk, now RSPB reserves. The number of breeding birds has slowly built up; on Havergate Island, however, the breeding success fluctuates markedly because of changes in the amount of food for the chick—mainly *Corophium*, a small crustacean—which is affected by both water levels and salinity. In a good year, around 150 pairs nest in Britain.

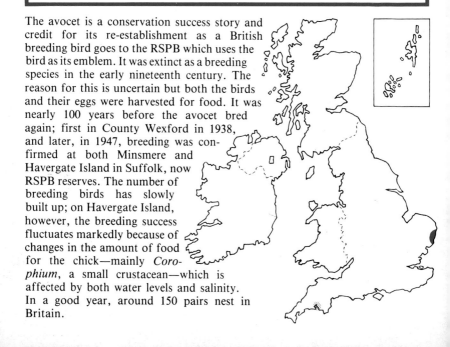

Great Skua

Stercorarius skua

Size: 20–23½ in (51–60 cm).

Recognition: large, heavily-built bird; dark brown all over except for distinct white flashes on both upper and lower sides of wing. Frequently seen chasing other seabirds.

Voice: mainly in display on breeding grounds, loud 'hah hah hah'.

Nesting: on moorland in loose groups. Nest is grass-lined cup on ground. 2 eggs incubated by both sexes for 28–30 days. Chicks fledge in about 6 to 7 weeks.

Feeding: mainly fish, often taken from other seabirds, and birds themselves; also scavenge on tideline.

Great skua (right) chasing herring gull.

A fearless bird, the great skua or bonxie, as it is called in Shetland, defends its nest with utmost ferocity. Intruders are dive-bombed and may be actually struck on the head. The skua also uses its size to intimidate other seabirds, making them regurgitate fish they have caught (kleptoparasitism). Piracy of this kind naturally leads to predation and great skuas kill many adult puffins and also take young birds, such as kittiwakes, from the nest. Great skuas first bred in Britain in 1774 (Shetland) but numbers only increased slowly during the nineteenth century, sustained by protection in some areas. A considerable increase and spread has occurred this century, and in 1974/75 there were about 6000 breeding pairs in Britain.

Arctic Skua

Stercorarius parasiticus

Size: 16–20 in (41–51 cm).

Recognition: smaller, slimmer build than great skua. 2 phases: both dark above but light phase has pale belly and throat, dark phase is brown all over. In flight, long slender wings with small wing-flashes; central tail feathers protrude slightly.

Voice: miaowing cry on breeding grounds—'ka-aaow'.

Nesting: on moorland in loose colonies. Nest is bare scrape on ground. 2 eggs incubated for 24 to 28 days by both sexes. Young fledge in about 4 weeks.

Feeding: inland, small mammals, birds and their eggs; at sea, fish obtained by kleptoparasitism.

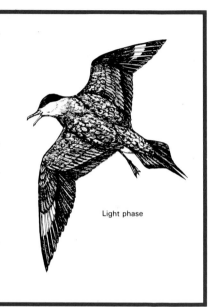

Light phase

Arctic skuas are even more piratical than the great skua, sometimes pursuing birds far larger than themselves, but concentrating on kittiwakes and terns. To watch a skua chasing an Arctic tern is particularly breath-taking; it follows every twist and turn until the tern finally disgorges its meal, the skua often catching the food before it hits the sea. The dark phase and an intermediate one are the most common in Britain where they blend well with heather. Breeding numbers appear to have declined on the Scottish mainland and the Hebrides during the nineteenth century, but are now more or less stable. Numbers have increased and the bird has spread in both Orkney and Shetland, the strongholds of the species in Britain. A survey in 1974/75 showed the British population to be about 2500 pairs.

Great Black-backed Gull

Larus marinus

Size: 26–29½ in (66–75 cm).

Recognition: very large gull; dark grey back, darker than lesser black-backed, with flesh-pink legs. Brown flecking on head of adults in winter. In flight, slow regular wing-beats with long glides.

Voice: deep hoarse 'agh-agh-agh' and barking 'aouk' calls.

Nesting: scattered colonies or solitary, on stacks or islands. Nest on ground, often close to wall or rocks used as vantage point. Usually 3 eggs incubated for 26–28 days by both sexes.

Feeding: mammals, other seabirds, eggs and young; also fish and invertebrates.

Adult

Immature

This is the largest gull nesting in Britain and Ireland and also the most predatory, with rabbits, puffins, Manx shearwaters and even sickly lambs all taken. Great black-backed gulls have increased since the beginning of the century but still remain the most scarce of the large gulls; numbers have been estimated at about 22 000 pairs. They are coastal breeders, although a few individuals do nest inland near lakes. One of the most remarkable features of their distribution is the almost complete lack of breeding birds from Berwick in the north, down the east coast to the Isle of Wight in the south. This is probably due to the lack of rocky cliffs and islands which they prefer. Adult breeding birds winter near the breeding grounds but immature and juvenile birds move south to the coast of Iberia.

Lesser Black-backed Gull

Larus fuscus

Size: 21½ in (55 cm).

Recognition: slate-grey mantle and yellow legs; dark edges to underwing show when bird takes off. Immature birds speckled brown, slightly darker than immature herring gull.

Voice: various calls: 'keew' and 'hahaha' most common, deeper and louder than herring gull.

Nesting: in colonies, usually with herring gulls, on flat grassy areas. Usually 3 eggs incubated by both birds for 26–28 days.

Feeding; marine feeder while breeding, especially fish; also small mammals, chicks, eggs, vegetable matter and carrion.

Winter plumage

In winter and during passage the British lesser black-backed gulls are joined by birds of the Scandinavian race which have a very much darker back, easily distinguished from the slate grey of the British race. Our own race used to be a migrant species, breeding here and wintering in Iberia and west Africa. Now considerable numbers stay, apparently surviving on what they can scavenge from rubbish dumps. When breeding in mixed colonies with herring gulls, the lesser black-backs prefer flatter areas whereas the herring gulls nest on the cliffs. Lesser black-backs also occur in greater numbers inland. In general, they have been increasing in Britain and Ireland, except in Orkney and Shetland where they complete with great black-backed gulls and great skuas. The total population in 1970 was estimated at around 47 000 pairs.

122

Herring Gull

Larus argentatus

Size: 22–23½ in (56–60 cm).

Recognition: silver-grey mantle, flesh-coloured legs and yellow bill; slightly larger than lesser black-backed gull. In flight black wing-tips seen from both above and below. Immatures speckled brown; very similar to lesser black-backs.

Voice: wide range of calls, one of commonest being 'keew-keew-keew'.

Nesting: in colonies mainly on rocky cliffs but also on dunes and even buildings. Large nest of weeds and grass. 3 eggs incubated for 25–27 days by both birds.

Feeding: young birds, eggs, small mammals, fish, offal, grain.

The herring gull has adapted well to man's lifestyle. It is the main scavenger around rubbish dumps and harbours, and also uses window ledges and chimney pots as nest-sites. Studies on the island of Skokholm, South Wales, showed that the birds which fed their young on food scavenged from the fish docks bred more successfully than those which mainly fed at sea. In 1970 the population was 335 000 pairs, and it has been increasing dramatically since the 1940s, the present growth rate being about 14 per cent per annum. They do not move far in winter and return as early as February to their breeding grounds. In some areas there is serious competition for space with other seabirds—on the Isle of May in the Firth of Forth the gulls have ousted the terns, and in other areas they have eroded the grassland where puffins, Manx shearwaters and storm petrels breed.

124

Black-headed Gull

Larus ridibundus

Size: 14–15½ in (36–39 cm).

Recognition: dark chocolate-brown head in summer with red legs and bill. In winter, white head with grey smudge behind eye. In flight, black wing-tips with white wedge along outer edgeof wings distinctive at all times.

Voice: harsh 'kwarr' or short 'kek'; bedlam of noise at breeding colonies.

Nesting: colonial on saltmarshes and sand dunes, also inland by marshy lakes. Nest is usually on ground. 3 eggs incubated for 22–24 days by both parents.

Feeding: wide range including offal, earthworms, insects and fish.

Breeding plumage

Winter plumage

The black-headed gull is an extremely successful bird and is as common on playing fields, rubbish dumps, suburban gardens and even following the plough, as on the coast. It was once rare in the London area, but now in winter about 200 000 roost on reservoirs there. The reason for this dramatic increase is due to the gulls' ability to adapt and use to advantage the changes brought about by man. The size of the breeding colonies can vary from less than a dozen pairs to 20 000 pairs at Needs Oar Point in Hampshire; the majority, however, contain less than 100 pairs. Only the coastal birds were counted in Operation Seafarer and these numbered about 75 000 pairs but the total population is somewhere between 150 000 and 300 000 pairs. The birds are relatively sedentary, but after breeding they move inland to urban areas.

Common Gull

Larus canus

> *Size:* 16–18 in (41–46 cm).
>
> *Recognition:* small gull with blue-grey back; yellow bill and greenish legs. Rounded head and dark eye give more gentle appearance than other gulls. In flight, long-winged, with white tips to black ends.
>
> *Voice:* notes higher pitched than other gulls; commonest call shrill 'kyow'.
>
> *Nesting:* both inland and on the coast, usually in small colonies. Nest varies from scrape to bulky seaweed and grass structure. Usually 3 eggs incubated for 24–26 days by both partners.
>
> *Feeding:* inland: earthworms, insects and seeds; on coast: marine invertebrates, fish and carrion.

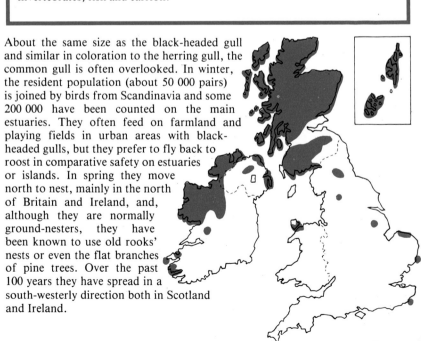

About the same size as the black-headed gull and similar in coloration to the herring gull, the common gull is often overlooked. In winter, the resident population (about 50 000 pairs) is joined by birds from Scandinavia and some 200 000 have been counted on the main estuaries. They often feed on farmland and playing fields in urban areas with black-headed gulls, but they prefer to fly back to roost in comparative safety on estuaries or islands. In spring they move north to nest, mainly in the north of Britain and Ireland, and, although they are normally ground-nesters, they have been known to use old rooks' nests or even the flat branches of pine trees. Over the past 100 years they have spread in a south-westerly direction both in Scotland and Ireland.

Kittiwake

Rissa tridactyla

Size: 18 in (46 cm).

Recognition: small gull; light grey mantle, yellow bill, black legs and dark eye. In flight, black triangular tips to wings, lacks white 'mirrors' of common gull. Immature well marked with dark 'V' across wings, dark band on neck and on tip of tail.

Voice: main call in colonies onomatopoeic 'kitti-wa-a-k'; rather silent away from nest.

Breeding: crowded cliff ledges; nest of seaweed cemented to ledge with guano. Usually 2 eggs incubated for 26–28 days by both partners.

Feeding: fish and marine invertebrates.

Most maritime of the gulls, the kittiwakes only comes to land to breed, and in the last 40 years have moved nearer human habitation, nesting on the window ledges of warehouses and other buildings. Along the River Tyne, kittiwakes use warehouses some 10½ miles (17 km) upriver in Newcastle and Gateshead. Kittiwakes have been increasing at a rate of 4 per cent per annum and Operation Seafarer estimated the British and Irish population to be just under 500 000 pairs. One of the reasons for this dramatic population growth is increased protection over the last century. In the 1800s kittiwakes were shot for sport and the juveniles were collected for their feathers which were used in the millinery trade. Birds were gathered from Lundy Island, Devon, and there are records of 700 being taken in a day.

Sandwich Tern

Sterna sandvicensis

Size: 15–17 in (38–43 cm).

Recognition: largest breeding tern. Shaggy black crest of elongated crown feathers gives head square appearance; black bill with yellow tip; black legs. In flight, long, thin wings and shorter tail than other terns.

Voice: noisy with loud grating 'kirrik' call.

Nesting: in colonies on sand dunes or shingle banks. 1 or 2 eggs incubated for about 25 days by both sexes. Young fledge in about 4 weeks but parental care may continue for 4 months.

Feeding: mainly fish taken by diving from height.

Crest

The loud, grating call of the Sandwich tern is normally heard before the bird is actually seen. In spring they perform spectacular aerial displays, ascending to great heights, then gliding down, calling. Sandwich terns often nest close to common or Arctic terns or even black-headed gulls, and they benefit from the aggression the other species show towards intruders. Great care must be taken when visiting a Sandwich tern colony as they can often desert the area completely, particularly at the beginning of the season and even when eggs have been laid. They may then eventually set up another colony as far away as 62 miles (100 km) from the original site. About 12 000 pairs breed in Britain and Ireland, and then migrate south to the coast of west Africa.

Common Tern

Sterna hirundo

Size: 14–15½ in (36–39 cm).

Recognition: red bill with black tip; red legs. Very similar to Arctic tern but tail streamers do not project beyond tips of closed wings when on ground; in flight, narrow dark patch near wing-tip.

Voice: long, grating 'kree-ee' which, with practice, can be distinguished from Arctic tern.

Nesting: in colonies on sand or shingle beaches; also inland. Nest is simple scrape. 2 or 3 eggs incubated by both parents for about 24 days. Young fledge in about 4 weeks.

Feeding: mainly fish, also crustaceans and marine worms, taken by diving.

Tail streamers

Tail streamers

The common tern is a more southerly breeding tern than the Arctic, but in Britain their ranges overlap and they often nest together. Common outnumber Arctic in most areas, but in the north and west of Scotland the reverse is true. Common terns feed nearer the coast and therefore take more insects and crustaceans than the Arctic. The colonies of inland-nesting common terns are always fairly small, but in Scotland and England, particularly the eastern counties, the habit has increased. This may be due to the increase in numbers of gravel pits where islands and rafts are often constructed. Common terns decreased during the 1800s, being used for sport, food and the millinery trade. The population reached a peak in about the 1930s and has since declined, numbers now being between 15 000 and 20 000 pairs.

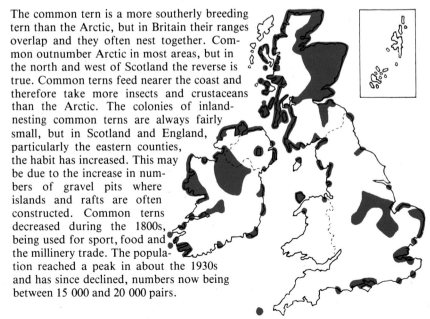

Arctic Tern

Sterna paradisaea

Size: 14–16½ in (36–42 cm).

Recognition: dark red bill and legs. Long tail streamers which project beyond wings when resting. In flight, translucent-looking wings distinguish it from common tern; also appears shorter necked with more rounded head.

Tail streamers

Voice: loud, screaming 'kee-yair' with emphasis on second syllable.

Nesting: in colonies on shingle or sand bank by coast. Nest is sparsely lined scrape on ground. 2 to 3 eggs incubated by both parents for 22 days.

Feeding: mainly sand eels, small herrings and sprats taken by diving.

The Arctic tern is one of the bird world's long-distance travellers, averaging 20 000 miles (32 000 km) a year in migration alone. Breeding sometimes as far north as the Arctic, it flies down to the Antarctic to winter and therefore lives through more daylight than any other bird in the world. There is evidence that these birds have retreated from their more southerly breeding areas; they used to outnumber the common tern in the Scilly Isles but now they do not breed there. Improvement in the climate during the first part of this century is one suggested cause. The stronghold of the Arctic tern is the north and west of Scotland, especially Orkney, and the total breeding population in Britain and Ireland is between 40 000 and 50 000 pairs. The oldest known Arctic tern lived 27 years.

136

Roseate Tern

Sterna dougallii

Size: 14–16½ in (36–42 cm).

Recognition: pale grey above,
very white below; breast has
slightly rosy tinge in spring;
bill almost black with red base.
In flight, long tail streamers
and whiteness are identifying
features.

Voice: long rasping 'aak aak'
call; also softer 'chuvick' when
carrying fish.

Nesting: in colonies usually on
islands. Nest is well concealed in
vegetation or rock crevice. 1
or 2 eggs incubated by both birds
for 23–25 days. Young fledge
in about 4 weeks.

Feeding: fish taken by diving;
also rob other terns of food.

Tail streamers

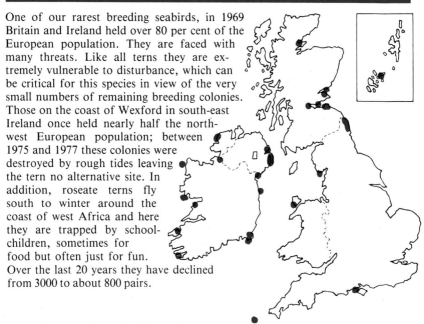

One of our rarest breeding seabirds, in 1969
Britain and Ireland held over 80 per cent of the
European population. They are faced with
many threats. Like all terns they are extremely vulnerable to disturbance, which can
be critical for this species in view of the very
small numbers of remaining breeding colonies.
Those on the coast of Wexford in south-east
Ireland once held nearly half the north-
west European population; between
1975 and 1977 these colonies were
destroyed by rough tides leaving
the tern no alternative site. In
addition, roseate terns fly
south to winter around the
coast of west Africa and here
they are trapped by schoolchildren, sometimes for
food but often just for fun.
Over the last 20 years they have declined
from 3000 to about 800 pairs.

Little Tern

Sterna albifrons

Size: 8½–10 in (22–25 cm).

Recognition: smallest tern; yellow bill with black tip, yellow legs, incomplete black cap as forehead is white. Dark grey leading edge to upper wing. Flight more fluttering and hurried than other terns.

Voice: high-pitched 'kik kik kik' call.

Nesting: in small colonies on shingle or sand beaches. Nest is simple, unlined scrape. 2 to 3 eggs incubated by both birds for 19–22 days. Young fly after less than 3 weeks.

Feeding: variable; small fish, crustaceans and marine worms taken by diving.

The little tern causes much concern to conservationists. It nests in widely spaced colonies very near to the high tide line where strong winds or high tides can completely destroy the nests. They also compete with holiday makers, choosing the same beaches that humans select. People walking through the colony sometimes trample the very well-camouflaged eggs or cause them to be chilled. Some nesting sites are now fenced off and many are wardened; these efforts are increasing the breeding success and number of birds nesting. However, these rather high concentrations can attract predators such as foxes, stoats and mink. Like other terns, the little tern probably reached a peak in numbers in the 1930s. By 1967 the species had declined to 1600 pairs and now numbers about 1800.

Razorbill

Alca torda

Size: 16 in (41 cm)

Recognition: stout, black and white auk with upright stance like penguin; deep, laterally compressed bill with vertical white stripe, also white stripe from bill to eye. Swift flight on whirring wings.

Voice: deep grating 'karrr'; noisy in colonies.

Nesting: crevices and cracks of cliff face in smaller colonies than guillemots. 1 egg incubated by both parents for about 35 days. Young leave nest-site at dusk some 18 days after hatching.

Feeding: small fish, mainly sand eels; also crustaceans and molluscs caught by diving from surface.

Razorbills avoid competition with guillemots by choosing slightly different sites on the cliff —areas where the face has crevices and is broken by scree, under and between boulders and occasionally in shallow earth burrows. They are quicker to take advantage of a new habitat; on Skokholm, South Wales, they even nested on a heap of coal. Razorbills return to the breeding cliffs in about March or April. The British and Irish population was estimated by Operation Seafarer to total about 144 000 pairs, representing about 70 per cent of the world population. Since the beginning of this century there has been a decline in numbers along the south coast; human pressure, oil and other pollutants most probably have been the causes. Oil pollution now poses an even greater threat both at the colonies and out at sea where the birds winter.

Guillemot

Uria aalge

Size: 16½ in (42 cm).

Recognition: auk with a slimmer build than razorbill; head, neck and back browny black, underparts white; slender, pointed bill. In flight, distinguished from razorbill by slimmer head profile.

Voice: silent except when breeding, then growling 'arrr' of varying pitch.

Nesting: on crowded cliff ledges, mainly in very large colonies. No nest. 1 egg incubated for about 33 days by both birds. Young leave nest-site when 18–25 days old.

Feeding: fish, mainly sprats; also crustaceans, worms and molluscs caught by diving from

Some guillemots have a 'bridled' marking running back from the eye—a genetic variation more common in birds from the north of the range. Its egg is pyriform (pear-shaped), and this is a special adaptation so that the egg always rolls round its centre of gravity when disturbed rather than off the ledge. Like the razorbill, guillemot chicks 'fledge' at night, to avoid predation by gulls, gliding to the sea on stubby, undeveloped wings; their parents are already at sea and keep in contact by calling frantically. The young birds will not return until two or more years later when they are ready to breed. Operation Seafarer estimated the British and Irish population to be about 577 000 pairs. Although colonies have declined markedly in the south, elsewhere the population seems to be holding its own, despite oil pollution.

Black Guillemot

Cepphus grylle

Size: 13½ in (34 cm).

Recognition: conspicuous white wing-patches on all-black body; bright red feet and gape. Smaller auk than guillemot and razorbill and crouches more when resting on land.

Voice: high-pitched 'sphee-ee-ee'.

Nesting: in holes, crevices or caves at bottom of cliffs. 2 eggs incubated for about 29 days by both parents. Chicks fledge when about 5–6 weeks old.

Feeding: fish, mainly butterfish; also crustaceans, molluscs and seaweed, taken by diving from surface in fairly shallow water.

Winter plumage

The black guillemot is often known by its Norse name, tystie. This bird differs from the other auks in that it lays two rather than one egg. They do not venture far from their colonies even in mid-winter and in early spring they gather in small groups on the sea at the bottom of cliffs. Here they perform communal displays, dancing on the water and chasing each other underwater, showing off their white wing-patches and red legs. Tysties are more restricted in their distribution than the rest of the auks and, during Operation Seafarer, 8340 pairs were counted. There appear to have been some declines in Scotland and in 1979 it was estimated that an oil spill in Shetland killed 16 per cent of the islands' population. It has recently recolonised Anglesey.

Puffin

Fratercula arctica

Size: 12–15½ in (30–39 cm).

Recognition: auk with a multicoloured, triangular bill of blue, red and yellow which is unmistakable; black above and white belly, orange legs. In winter, bill loses its bright colours; immatures also have duller bill. In flight, very fast wing-beats.

Voice: deep, purring 'aar'.

Nesting: in colonies in burrows on grassy cliff tops or islands. 1 egg incubated for about 42 days by both parents. After being fed for about 6 weeks by parents, young is deserted; leaves burrow about 10 days later.

Feeding: fish, mainly sand eels and sprats, taken by diving from surface.

The puffin is one of the best-known seabirds. With its short dumpy wings, it seems very clumsy as it comes in to land or is taking off. However, it is beautifully adapted for swimming underwater, using its wings as paddles. In the eighteenth and nineteenth centuries puffins were harvested for food and feathers on the islands of St Kilda, but the colonies seem to have remained stable. Numbers have declined in the south since the beginning of the twentieth century, but recent studies have shown they are increasing slightly in the north-west and rapidly in the north-east. On the Isle of May in the Firth of Forth, for example, only a few pairs nested up until the 1960s, but in 1975 over 3000 were breeding. Total population figures are given rather conservatively at 500 000.

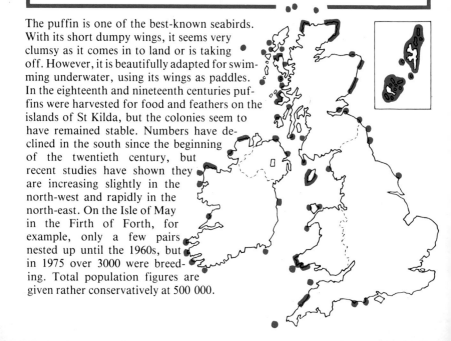

Rock Pipit

Anthus spinoletta

Size: 6½ in (17 cm).

Recognition: passerine with olive-grey back, darkish streaked breast, dark legs; blends well with rocks. In flight, outer tail feathers are dusky, not pure white as with other pipits. Juvenile more streaked than adult bird.

Voice: 'tseep' call when taking off and in flight.

Nesting: holes or crevices behind rock. Nest built by female of grasses and lined with feathers. 4–5 eggs incubated by hen for about 14 days. Young fed by both parents and fly at 16 days.

Feeding: insects, slugs, worms, snails, crustaceans and some vegetable matter.

Rock pipits are mainly found on rocky coasts. They feed among seaweed, taking huge numbers of larvae and flies; a study in the south-west of England showed that they consumed slightly more than their own weight each day. In winter a few birds sometimes move inland and are found round sewage farms and watercress beds. At this time the resident population is joined by birds from Scandinavia, which are a different race and in spring can be distinguished by their eyestripe and pinkish chin. The population of rock pipits seems to have remained unchanged for several generations. However, from about 1880, the Sussex population became extinct for 40 years but re-established themselves in the 1930s. The suggested British and Irish population is over 50 000 pairs.

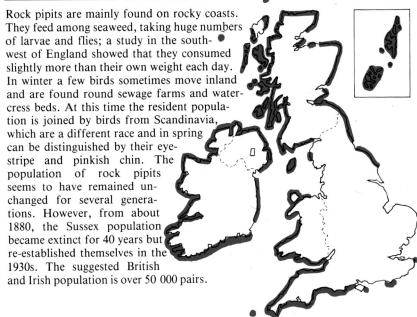

The Future

In these pages, we have seen something of the incredible diversity and richness of our coastal bird fauna, noting in passing how our estuaries and coasts are of international importance for the hundreds of thousands of shorebirds and wildfowl they support on passage and in winter, and remarking, too, on the importance of our huge seabird colonies—which probably hold over $5\frac{1}{2}$ million seabirds in all. The map on page 000 shows how various conservation bodies have established a network of vital reserves around the coasts of Britain and Ireland; more are in the pipeline, and as we write this we hear of proposals to establish marine nature reserves in the United Kingdom under the new Wildlife and Countryside Bill. Some species are increasing—notably kittiwake and gannets—and well-organised protection and conservation efforts are benefiting various others and their habitats. Direct human persecution is scarcely a factor where most species are concerned. Everything might seem rosy . . . but is this really the case? Sadly, we have to conclude that it is not.

Traditionally, the sea has provided man with a vast dustbin for all kinds of his refuse, not necessarily always to the detriment of its wildlife. Today, however, the waste products of an increasingly technological society are giving cause for serious concern. Industrial waste in the form of various toxic chemicals—most notably the polychlorinated biphenyls (PCBs), heavy metals and pesticide residues—is finding its way into the marine environment at an alarming rate, often concentrating in birds at the top of food chains and causing debilitation, infertility and death.

Oil is probably the best-known pollutant, especially following such well-publicised tanker disasters as those involving the *Torrey Canyon*, the *Christos Bitas*, the *Esso Bernica* and the *Amoco Cadiz*. Huge oil slicks have had deadly effects on both wintering and breeding seabirds, killing large numbers of birds inshore, out to sea or, as was the case with the *Esso Bernica* in Shetland, at an oil terminal. Just as serious, and far more difficult to detect and control, are the endless small spillages at sea, the jettison of waste oil and the dumping of ballast water mixed with oil. Notwithstanding internationally agreed rules and tremendous efforts by conservationists (and, it must be said, by some oil companies and other agencies), the oil pollution problem is still very much with us and, at times, one could be forgiven for thinking that the main concern of the powers that be is this or that bathing beach or holiday coast, rather than the marine environment and its wildlife.

Fortunately, most seabird colonies are not at risk from most of man's activities—oil exploitation excluded. Development for industry, agriculture or recreation does not affect the rockier coasts of the north and west to the same extent as it does our estuaries and low-lying coasts. All too often, man's attitude to these latter, very important areas is that they are 'wastelands' which ought to be reclaimed or 'developed' in some way. Urbanisation and industry have not always adversely affected estuaries and tidal river systems: very often they are concentrated in relatively small areas and very often a proportion of the coastal bird population comes to terms with them to some degree. Inevitably, however, the demand for more and more development threatens the best remaining natural sites on many estuaries, be it for more factories, port developments, housing, marinas, agricultural expansion or whatever. Some complete estuary systems are now threatened with the installation of barrages—such as Morecambe Bay, The Wash, the Severn and even the Thames. A recent *cause célèbre*, the controversy over the use of Maplin Sands on the Essex coast for London's third airport, possibly did more to focus attention on the loss of coastal wildlife habitats of international importance than any other, but—ironically—Maplin has been spared (temporarily) on economic rather than conservation grounds.

Habitat loss is critical and, for many coastal birds, irreversible. Fortunately, we in Britain and Ireland have a team of professional, articulate and well-supported conservationists, tirelessly working to preserve the best of our wildlife habitats for posterity, and endeavouring to show that the multi-purpose use of coastlines, if well-planned and based on a broad-minded approach, can actually work—to man's ultimate advantage. Unhappily, theirs is always an uphill struggle, often against sectional interests and the doctrines of short-term expediency and gain. To them, the future remains uncertain, but they remain optimistic!

You can find out more about conservation, and how you can help, from the various organisations we have listed on pages 43—45.

The Birdwatchers' Code of Conduct

This code has been drafted after consultation between the British Ornithologists' Union, the British Trust for Ornithology, the Royal Society for the Protection of Birds, the Scottish Ornithologists' Club, the Wildfowl Trust and the Editors of British Birds.

Today's birdwatchers are a powerful force for nature conservation. The number of those of us interested in birds rises continually and it is vital that we take seriously our responsibility to avoid any harm to birds. We must also present a responsible image to non-birdwatchers who may be affected by our activities and particularly those on whose sympathy and support the future of birds may rest.

There are 10 points to bear in mind:
1. The welfare of birds must come first.
2. Habitat must be protected.
3. Keep disturbance to birds and their habitat to a minimum.
4. When you find a rare bird, think carefully about whom you should tell.
5. Do not harass rare migrants.
6. Abide by the Bird Protection Acts at all times.
7. Respect the rights of landowners.
8. Respect the rights of other people in the countryside.
9. Make your records available to the local bird recorder.
10. Behave abroad as you would when birdwatching at home.

Welfare of birds must come first
Whether your particular interest is photography, ringing, sound recording, scientific study or just birdwatching, remember that the welfare of the bird must always come first.

Habitat protection
Its habitat is vital to a bird and therefore we must ensure that our activities do not cause damage.

Keep disturbance to a minimum

Birds' tolerance of disturbance varies between species and seasons. Therefore, it is safer to keep *all* disturbance to a minimum. No birds should be disturbed from the nest in case opportunities for predators to take eggs or young are increased. In very cold weather, disturbance to birds may cause them to use vital energy at a time when food is difficult to find. Wildfowlers already impose bans during cold weather: birdwatchers should exercise similar discretion.

Rare breeding birds

If you discover a rare bird breeding and feel that protection is necessary, inform the appropriate RSPB Regional Office, or the Species Protection Department at the RSPB's Headquarters. Otherwise, it is best in almost all circumstances to keep the record strictly secret in order to avoid disturbance by other birdwatchers and attacks by egg-collectors. Never visit known sites of rare breeding birds unless they are adequately protected. Even your presence may give away the site to others and cause so many other visitors that the birds may fail to breed successfully.

Disturbance at or near the nest of species listed on the First Schedule of the Protection of Birds Act, 1954 is a criminal offence.

Rare migrants

Rare migrants or vagrants must not be harassed. If you discover one, consider the circumstances carefully before telling anyone. Will an influx of birdwatchers disturb the bird or others in the area? Will the habitat be damaged? Will problems be caused with the landowner?

Protection of Birds Acts

The bird protection laws are the result of hard campaigning by previous generations of birdwatchers. As birdwatchers, we must abide by these laws at all times and not allow them to fall into disrepute.

Respect the rights of landowners

The wishes of landowners and occupiers of land must be respected. Do not enter land without permission. Comply with permit schemes. If you are leading a group, do give advance notice of the visit, even if a formal permit scheme is not in operation. Always obey the Country Code.

Respect the rights of other people

Have proper consideration for other birdwatchers. Try not to disrupt their activities or scare the birds they are watching. There are many other people who also use the countryside. Do not interfere with their activities and, if it seems that what they are doing is causing unnecessary disturbance of birds, do try to take a balanced view. Flushing gulls when walking a dog on a beach may do little harm, while the same dog might be a serious disturbance at a tern colony. When pointing this out to a non-birdwatcher, be courteous, but firm. The non-birdwatchers' goodwill towards birds must not be destroyed by the attitudes of birdwatchers.

Keeping records

Much of today's knowledge about birds is the result of meticulous record-keeping by our predecessors. Make sure you help to add to tomorrow's knowledge by sending records to your county bird recorder.

Birdwatching abroad

Behave abroad as you would at home. This code should be firmly adhered to when abroad (whatever the local laws). Well-behaved birdwatchers can be important ambassadors for bird protection.

Glossary

Auk: small- to medium-sized diving seabird of the Family *Alcidae.*

Corvid: bird of the crow family (*Corvidae*).

Deposition: the process of laying down of materials—in our context, by the sea.

Depredation: the act of preying upon other species.

Dinoflagellates: tiny, primitive animals (or plants, according to some) which move by means of two minute, threadlike organs.

Diver: medium-large swimming and diving bird of the Family *Gaviidae.*

Duck: web-footed swimming birds of the Family *Anatidae,* some of which dive underwater.

Eclipse plumage: the plumage of ducks at the time of their annual moult, during part of which they are flightless.

Estuary: the area—usually broad and flat—at a river mouth where it meets the sea.

Fledge: strictly, to become feathered, but also loosely used to denote the act of leaving the nest.

Gape: the inside of a bird's mouth at the base of the bill.

Genotype: basic genetic construction of an organism.

Goose: medium-sized, web-footed swimming bird of the Family *Anatidae,* usually larger and more terrestrial than duck.

Interglacial period: the period between two Ice Ages.

Intertidal zone: the area between high and low watermark of tides, exposed at low tide, covered at high tide.

Kleptoparasitism: the act of robbing another animal of its prey or food.

Longshore drift: the process whereby a beach grows laterally, caused by deposition of material as the tide strikes it obliquely before running off again at right angles to it.

Machair: fertile land based on shell-sand, mainly confined to the Hebrides and parts of western Ireland.

Marram: a tough, sand-growing grass—*Ammophila*—especially on dunes.

Passerine: a perching bird of the Order Passeriformes, e.g., crow, finch, thrush, warbler, tit, etc.

Pleistocene: the most recent geological period, which lasted for one million years; it is the period from which most fossils are known, and ended with the last Ice Age.

Race: geographical form of a

species; a subspecies.

Reclamation: the 'recovery' of any land by man, usually from the sea, water, marshland, etc., for agricultural or industrial development.

Salinity: salt content, e.g., of water or soil.

Sand: aggregation of tiny mineral particles—larger than silt, smaller than in shingle.

Shell-sand: resembles sand in appearance, but is made up of tiny particles of shells.

Shingle: aggregation of small stones and pebbles, usually worn smooth and rounded by water action.

Silt: minute particles of mineral matter, etc.; much finer-grained than sand.

'True' seabird: a bird which feeds and lives mainly or exclusively at sea, coming ashore only to breed.

Tube-nose: a bird, e.g., fulmar, with the nostrils situated 'externally' in a tube lying on the top of the bill.

Wader: bird which mainly frequents shallow water habitats, either coastal or inland, and which is a member of one of the following Families: *Charadriidae* (plovers), *Haematopodidae* (oystercatchers), *Scolopacidae* (snipe, curlews, godwits, sandpipers, etc.), *Recurvirostridae* (avocets and stilts), *Phalaropodidae* (phalaropes), *Burhinidae* (stone-curlews) and *Glareolidae* (coursers and pratincoles).

Waterfowl: a fairly inexact term: unlike wildfowl, which usually covers geese, swans and duck only, waterfowl can mean any swimming birds, i.e., wildfowl plus grebes, divers, coots, etc.

Index